LET HER BE LOUD

MARJIE MONRO

D1519200

For every person that has ever felt like a tender sprout striving to split the earth in order to bloom — I see you. May this book reach you like a hug or like a whisper that says, you are allowed.

And for my Mama — may the light find you. May it break open the rusted hinges of the armor you wear so fiercely. May someone hold you — skin to skin — nurture the baby girl inside of you. May you find the courage to heal, and the will to love.

PROLOGUE

I hope this book crawls into your body and I hope it lives under your skin. Just for a little while. I hope it takes you somewhere and I hope that when you come back - you have had the feeling of knowing someone deeply and of being known deeply. Because — correct me if i'm wrong, isn't that what we all long for in the end? To know and be known in our nakedness. I hope you embrace the discomfort like a hug, or like being wrapped inside your favorite sweater, knowing, or perhaps learning, that discomfort is not an enemy. I have laid myself bare here. Into every word, I have sought to breathe a heartbeat. Can you hear it? It is thumping steadily even now. Like a soft chant or like an invitation. It is my story, but I hope you can find a piece of yourself somewhere in these pages. As you feel, I hope you will also be felt.

I HAVE WRITTEN this is for the hidden places we are afraid to speak of, for the questions that demand to be asked, for all the things that were done in the darkness to finally belong in the light. This is for hope and darkness, newness and pain to breathe the same air, no longer afraid to exist together. This is to construct language for the cost of waking up and healing. This is for the wounding and the wounded.

LET'S BEGIN.

STALE TEA

I told myself I was a dreamer.
    I wanted to be, but it was a lie.
    I never let my thoughts mature into dreams.
    It seemed pointless.
    Foolish, even.

Then one night I slept and saw a vision:

Twin girls, one radiant and rich in color, the other black
    and white, but less defined, or maybe grey, like stale tea.
    The two stared at each other, assessing — scrutinizing everything
that was similar,
    the multitudes of differences in between.
    And the colorful girl said to the other,

"Aren't you tired of pretending I don't exist?
    I am so tired of sleeping."

The words jolted me violently out of sleep, my body sweating,
    my sheets coated in me. I walked languidly to the bathroom,
    splashed the cold water on my face, rubbing profusely.

And as I let my eyes glance upward toward the mirror,
    I noticed it —

One eye, once grey like stale tea,
    now brown like my favorite milk chocolate.

POISON

Your poison is my power
 Keeps words flowing out of my finger tips
 like bitter rivers
 Like sticky blood landing on pages
 disguised as something beautiful
 Like putrid open wounds
 manufactured into something palpable
 Who am I apart from the perverse melody of your scorn?
 A flightless bird
 Wings only fluttering when caught
 in the phantom whistle of your scorching hatred
 Voice vibrating only
 in the aftershock of your fury
 My story is you
 My words are you
 My tears, you
 You make me beautiful
 By stripping me of beauty
 Like a tall tree stripped naked
 by the trim fingers of winter
 Pretend death
 Only to thrive
 Clutching to the heels of dawn
 —

 Your poison is my power
 A self sustaining spring welling endlessly inside me
 Years of pretend death coaching me into
 Some kind force to be reckoned with
 Your poison is my power
 Until suddenly
 And in the end
 My power is your poison

PART I

Before I drifted off to sleep I always found myself uttering my hopes into the blank space. At the time I wouldn't have called them prayers. You have to believe in something in order to pray, it's a rule, and at the time the only thing I believed in was how much a person could hurt you. My hopes back then were simple: all I wanted was to wake up at my own volition. Not to the sound of her footsteps moving toward the bedroom door, not to her weight making a dent in my small body, not to the sound of my sister screaming. Later in life, when all the soot had finally been scoured from my body, I'd come to savor the mornings when I would sigh awake, let my eyes adjust to the sanctuary of my tiny home. I'd speak out into the light, this time little utterances of gratitude, always beginning with "hello, home."

But I am getting ahead of myself.

On that night, I closed my eyes and whispered into the blackness. I remember wanting to weep from the volume of silent hopes. If any part of it felt the most like bondage, it was this; the parts of me that insisted on believing there could be more than being scared, slithering and roaring inside me. I pulled the pillow from underneath my head and pressed it firmly into my face, pressing and pushing and willing those hopes into smothered submission, or myself to sleep, whichever happened first.

I dreamed of what it must feel like to laugh when you are free. What it must feel like to have the stronghold of fear unclasped from around your neck, your wrists, your entire body even, limbs creaking as they stretched outward and upward, that creaking the sound of newfound freedom. I dreamed of my daddy walking in the front door of that old townhouse, arms extended outward inviting me into the embrace I'd been waiting shamelessly for. I pressed my face into his white shirt, dug my fingers into his back; he still smelled the same. Even in my dreams I was weighed down with unspeakable hopes. This time they shouted, "let this be real, let this be real." And it was real. It was real until, on that day, my dreaming was pierced by familiar sounds, howls that reached inside greedily, ripping me from his arms. I think I collected some of his skin under my fingernails as souvenirs. It happened so suddenly, I didn't have time to grieve the loss of his arms around me.

By this time my ears were highly attuned to the sound an object makes when it connects with flesh. The sound the heel of a shoe makes, at first a whistle when flying backward, as if in warning, and then a sharp crack as it causes ripples against tender skin. These are not the sounds a person should have to become accustomed to, but I have learned that you don't choose all the lessons that you will eventually learn in this life.

My feet were moving before my eyes had fully opened, carrying me across the hall. I saw Her hovering there (I was right about the shoe, possibly I could have guessed the exact one from the other room, but this is not a particular skillset I wish to boast about) above my sister, now crouched on the floor. Her body was pressed into the carpet, arms up, eyes wide with fear. When I remember that moment my sister always seems so small. In fact in all my remembering, we always seem so small. It's puzzling because by that time, we were probably the same size as Her in stature. We could, perhaps, have used our alliance as sisters to attempt to subvert the autocracy with which she governed us. But terror, it is a powerful thing. It can trick you right out of believing that you are strong and big. It can steal your agency and your voice. It just paralyzes your awareness of yourself because there isn't room for you. There is only Her, and you just have to give all your energy to watching and waiting and staying one step ahead.

"Stop," I must have screamed, rushing over. I knew as I wrapped my hands around her thick arm what I was inviting, but by now my sister and I had mastered the ability to share the burden of pain. I don't remember the next part. Or perhaps I do, but I don't want to. I don't want to remember what she did next, I don't want to remember which parts of me hurt next, don't want to reacquaint myself with the sound of sole or fist or plastic against flesh. I don't want to remember the frenzy of limbs flying, the shouts, the accusations, the threats. I don't want to remember my sister's naked body, my mother shoving underwear down her throat to silence her. I don't want to remember

12

that this was all over a missing jacket. I don't want to remember. Don't make me remember the sound a voice makes when it is pleading in fear for it to stop, the ache of the heart to simply be believed for once.

AND THEN A CAR horn bellowing from our driveway. You will laugh when I tell you that even now I can remember the tone it made, clear and distinct, puncturing the chaos for just a moment. Her hand was still raised in the air but this time no sharp crack to follow. She ran back to her bedroom and fetched her things, late for work, her ride waiting. She pushed her head into the doorway one more time, hands haphazardly smoothing her wig back into it's place,

"If you don't find it before I get home, I will finish what I started. I will beat you through the night," she said. It turns out you don't need objects to cause someone's skin to shudder. Sometimes you just need words.

I have gone over this in my mind a million times, played it back, slowed it down, torn it to shreds. Sometimes I think maybe we could have stayed, maybe we could have survived the night. Maybe. But with our backs pressed into the edge of that bed, my baby sister cradled in my arms, I looked up at my big sister's face. I saw that her song of optimism had died. Her face frightened me, skin under eyes inflated. I wondered what she saw when she looked at me. I closed my eyes and listened for the roar of hopes, but there was nothing. There was nothing.

I had wanted to die so many times. I'd imagined all the ways I could do it without making a sound. I had wished I was strong enough to complete the task, fantasized about what stillness would feel like, how one quick slice could finally bring the peace I was famished for. My sister had gotten closer than me, swallowed pills, but not enough. Mum only chuckled when she discovered the empty bottle on the bathroom floor. Apparently not even the potential of death could soften her. But on that day, some stubborn streak slithered its way up from some unseen place inside me and I thought to myself, if I die it will be because I choose to die, not because she kills me. I didn't want this to be the way my life ended, crouched on the grey carpet in terror. The words I said next changed everything. I still wear those words as a cape of responsibility around my shoulders, those words, and worse, their consequences, constantly pulling me backwards into places I never intended for us to go. They turned us into orphans. They changed my sisters. They changed me. They left my mother barren, the fruit of her womb snatched out from under her. Sometimes I don't know if it was selfish.

Is it selfish to want to live?

"We can't stay here," I finally whispered, "she will kill us."

Possibly you are now shaking your head as you read this, unconvinced that life can hinge so desperately on the location of an article of clothing. I understand. It seems so insignificant, like nonsense, a jacket. Years later, she told my sister that she'd found the jacket on the back of her chair at the office. I don't know why she told her. Maybe it was the only version of an apology she could muster. Or maybe her insides required her to confess. I wish I could have watched that day unfold on split screens. Screen A: three girls fly about the house, opening drawers, craning their necks into corners and under beds, searching one more time just in case the jacket ended up in the wrong place at the last visit to the laundromat. Screen B: Mum walks into work, eyes land almost immediately on brown jacket hanging lazily on the back side of her chair. I wonder what mothers think about after they have left their children bleeding on the floor. Do they watch their fingers moving over their keyboards and feel disgusted that these very same hands could cause such damage? Do they spend the day swallowing back tears, their bodies awash with tremors of remorse? Do they? Do you think the sight of that jacket ignited the spark that would finally send blood pumping back to her heart?

If it did, she never let on.

Brows wet, we perched once more on the edge of the bed. Our hands were empty.

"We have to go," one of our voices sliced through the fog.

I descended the stairs to the main floor, picked up the phone and dialed the phone number of my german teacher. I spewed the whole story out in between gasps, my heart threatening to fly right out of my chest. She had heard these stories before. Had heard about the reports made about the closed door happenings of that townhouse. Children's services had come. They'd come and they'd left and more scars were added as a penalty.

"Please. Help us."

People will think leaving was an easy choice. I've been called brave for picking up the phone and calling for help. But sometimes people don't want to hear that bravery comes at a cost. Sometimes you are only brave because you have run out of options. Sometimes you are only brave because the part of you that has been waiting to be held has finally given up and now all that is left is survival. Sitting in that taxi, our shoulders pressed against each other, plastic bag of clothes limply in my lap, fist full of cash, I turned my head to look back. I let the tears I had been holding in drip down my face. We were escaping because we wanted to live, but we were also leaving our mother. Please don't miss this part, I beg. As I write this, over a decade later, I feel my heart constricting, the tears beginning to spill over. Even after all those years, I believed mum was in there somewhere. I wanted to stay just in case today might be the day I'd finally meet her. But, I confess, I wanted to stay alive even more. That is why I let myself take the cash from my school teacher and why I let her call a taxi to pick us up. It's why I didn't let myself think overlong about the consequences of what we were doing, how it might unloose one shackle only to tighten the grip of another.

The drive seemed to stretch on unnecessarily. I kept squeezing my sisters' hands to keep them from wailing. I couldn't deal with the sound of their own grief while trying to stay coherent. I was practicing what I had to make sure to tell whoever would be collecting our story. I could not be overly emotional in this case. The police had visited our house before. They'd seen my head sliced open. I was sure they could hear my bloody shirt crying out from the next room. They'd asked and I had fabricated some disorganized story about walking into a door foolishly, my eyes attempting to convey the truth without having to utter the words. I could feel her eyes examining me, scorching me in silent warning. The police left. So you understand why, on that car ride to the hospital, I forced my emotions back and made sure this time they would intervene. I had learned that police were not moved by emotion. They were not moved by blood. They were moved by logic. By facts.

I stuffed the cash in the taxi driver's hand. Then a whirlwind of arms and voices as we were ushered to separate rooms. I felt trapped in the blankness. Can someone explain to me the reason that hospital rooms are tinted in the most unnatural shade of white? Do you know? It is not for the benefit of the patient, I will tell you. You can hear your own heartbeat bouncing off corners that suddenly feel like they are pressing up against you. I focused on the doorknob, waiting and willing it to turn, until finally, one loud knock and a twist.

First a police officer, hatless, bald, asking me what happened. I told him the truth, but just the facts. I didn't cry, I didn't let my voice crack. I told him, "If you will not help us, then just take us home quietly before she returns from work. Because if she finds out we tried to escape, and then you take us home, she will kill us."

Now a social worker, kinky black hair, mustard dress, asking me the same questions. I told her wearily, "If you will not help us, then just take us home quietly before she returns from work. Because if she finds out we tried to escape she will kill us."

Now a man with a camera. He asked a different question, something about bruises and scars. He wanted his camera to capture the evidence of abuse. For this part, I could not keep my eyes from being a little bit wet. I steadied myself by breathing deeply and I showed him what was still visible. I wanted him to leave. I wanted to scream. I wanted to laugh. I wanted to hide underneath the paper covering the hospital table. I wanted to ask him to lay me down and cut me open in a straight line so he could get a full picture of the scars he was asking about. Not all forms of abuse are visible to the human eye. They cannot be developed in a dark room and printed on paper, you understand? And in any case, I am a black girl, in case you have forgotten by now. Bruises? You know, *black* and blue? Even those are camouflaged by nature. I wanted to throw his flashing camera against the nearly white walls. It was as if my pain was invisible, as if he was trying to distill thirteen years of abuse into a few pictures. But he was missing it. He was missing me. I let him finish and then I told him, "If you will not help us, then just take us home quietly before she returns from work. Because," and this time my voice did splinter slightly, "she will kill us."

ORDER

This wasn't always the order of things.
    Once your body kept me breathing, perhaps against your will.
    I fit neatly inside you— connected by more than invisible strings
—

    shared body; shared blood.
    I was undeniably yours then, a cord of flesh the proof.

But as you pushed me out — you wept a cry of liberation,
    a freedom from that type of closeness
    The type of nearness that mocked your icy demeanor,
    threatened your strength

One last push sent all your fears scampering back into their corners
    I wonder if they felt it too, as smooth metal sailed through arteries
    A severing of more than flesh.
    Your relief was audible—
    I'll keep her body, you recited to yourself—
    Everything else is too much trouble.

It had not always been this bad. What I mean is, it had not always felt this dire; it had always been bad. In the beginning there was Africa, thousands of miles away from the townhouse at the end of the road. Then there were only two of us girls, my older sister and I, at least for a little while. We were born less than two years apart. Whenever she was fed up with my pestering her, she'd tell the story of how she'd slapped my little face when I'd been born. She laughed spitefully as she told it, but I knew even as she said it, I was her best friend. She was mine too. She was bold and brave in every way that I wasn't, that was true when we were small, and remained so after we grew. We lived by different truths: she, knowing that life was painful, stubbornly faced it, determined to touch and taste and see every good adventure that was out there. I was a frightened and watchful child, constantly flinching. Daddy called me his little butter fingers. I broke plates and cups, the glass slipping out of my fingers as I jumped, my ears registering a car coming down the driveway or a door creaking open. I envied my big sister. Her charisma sourced itself in her open heart. Even when things were the darkest, she believed that there was good out there in the world. I walked just one step behind her, a little shadow, desperately hoping that if I stayed close enough, I'd soak up some of her light. I wanted to be just like her. I looked in the mirror and longed for her beauty, sucking in my nostrils to try and minimize the width of my broad nose. In a place where things seemed to change without warning, my sister was the one thing that stayed the same. We learned to speak without words, to make each other giggle in spite of it all, to dream, perhaps of a time when we would live together in our own tiny home, safe and free. We rode the swells of life together, spending our days being driven miles and miles up a winding road, singing along to Puff Daddy's "I'll be missing you." The two of us sang with the windows down, eyes squeezed shut with all our pent up passion and silliness. The closer to home we got, the louder we sang, the bigger we laughed until only one more twist in the road and we were home. Then silence. Always silence on that straight stretch to the front of our house.

Home was beautiful, grand even. I didn't know it then, but that much land meant you were special, privileged. When my parents were happy, and maybe even still a little in love, there was a bed of flowers that split the driveway in two, the centerpiece to a world stretching out in every direction. Green all over, with guava trees and peach trees, goats and wild dogs. We'd wander around and pluck the peaches off the trees too early and their fuzzy outsides would make our lips itch. I remember the taste of sugar cane against my tongue, my sister and I chomping away just as clumsily as those goats, palms callused, mouths raw and bloody.

The front of the house had two entrances. One door opened up into the kitchen, and the other into the ornately furnished sitting area where daddy entertained his friends and hosted his business colleagues. I knew that when he had people on that side of the house, we were to make ourselves scarce and play quietly. That was also the side of the house we would decorate at Christmas time. A huge Christmas tree would be hoisted up against the open window. Daddy would open bottles of champagne and sneak drips into our empty glasses, letting us giggle at the sensation of the popping bubbles. He would ask us, a tipsy twinkle in his eye, what we wanted Father Christmas to bring us.

"Makeup and chocolate," I always replied, a twinkle in my eyes to match his.

Through the middle of the sitting room, and up three useless stairs, another room with big leather chairs and a television against the wall. This is where daddy would retire at the end of the night when he was home, flip on the television and cheer on the football teams or watch the highlights from the day's news. In the day I would carry my rocks into this room and splay them on the carpet. I'd study them while soaking up the remnants of the energy he had left behind the night before. I liked to sit there in the silence. It made me feel close to him.

A long hallway divided the house in two. On the way to the other side was a guest bedroom and an accompanying full bathroom. That was the bathroom big sister and I had snuck off into to try one of Mum's hidden cigarettes. We lit it and pressed it into our lips, letting it hang there. I felt nothing and neither did she. We flushed it down the toilet shaking our heads in confusion about the reasons anyone would ever waste their time with one of those. Past the guest room, another little living room. This one was ours, small and concealed to keep our cartoons from floating down the hallway and interrupting grown up business. With the door closed to that room, big sister and I told secrets and danced to Whitney Houston. That was also the room where we waited, our knees pressed to our chests or our palms against our ears, for the sounds of Mum and Daddy fighting to stop. He'd come in when it was over and look into our crying faces and say cooly,

"I'm sorry girls," retrieve the shoe or utensils that had flown through the door during the madness, and march on.

We'd always start out at the sidelines of the kitchen, across the hall and through the double door, crying and screaming at them to stop. I'd wince as his fist connected with Mum's cheek. I'd look around trying to find an object I could throw at his head. Eventually the arms of one of our workers would land on our shoulders, slice through the fog and pull us away and into that little living room across the hall. I didn't want to remember them like this but the images kept dancing inside my mind as we waited.

Down the hall past the kitchen were the bedrooms. A Jack and Jill that my sisters and I shared, except for the nights when Mum took one room, refusing to share a bed with daddy. Finally, on the opposite side of the hall, their master bedroom sat like a wing of its own, a huge bed in the center. It was always a mystery to me why a man like Daddy would not make sure to come home to a room as grand as that. I was always an imaginative child. I could create worlds in my mind, rich and fully furnished, but I never could imagine a home more beautiful.

I am only saying all this so that we understand each other. I was born into the makings of what could have been a colorful and blissful childhood. On paper, I was lucky, born into a family of prominence, of wealth. But I'll tell you something, paper is just paper. It will not survive the reality of pain. When the pain comes, you cannot simply wave it away, as if your paper luck has enough power in the end. Don't misunderstand me, this paper power had its perks. My daddy was a politician, and sharing his last name meant going to church with the president and having our picture in the newspaper. It meant that birthdays were a sensation, presents stacked high, important people filling our driveway with their vehicles. I was never foolish enough to believe it was about me. This is one of those unsolicited lessons I spoke of earlier: when everyone knows your name, no one really knows you. And it was true. Our family was paper perfect, admired, respected. It was an adequate disguise for the things going on inside that house on the hill.

On the best days, we'd return home from school and find my dad's blue Mercedes parked at the front of the house. We'd look over at each other and let the air we'd been holding in whistle out through our teeth, a mixture of relief and trepidation. We'd throw open the car doors and run into the house, grab our roller blades and beg daddy to watch us race on the marble veranda where he'd taught us to keep our ankles sturdy, lean forward and trust that our feet would not come out from under us. It was as if, when he was home, I let parts of myself out into the world. As if pieces of me were released after years of necessary quarantining.

He was such a complex man, as if different souls fit neatly inside his body, taking turns making an appearance. On television he was always so serious, determined and passionate. I didn't understand then what he was so eager about, what larger mission fueled him with such unshakable commitment, but I would nod my head vehemently, attempting to mimic his passion. Then there was the man who came home to me. This man whose smile split open some tightly sealed cistern inside of me. He was full of silliness and gentleness, insisting on roasting an entire chicken for his dinner late at night, laughing as I pulled off his socks and tickled his feet. This was the man who was full of apologies and promises that one day he would not have to work so hard and be absent so often. I play these things on repeat so I don't lose track of them, to remind my mind that this is non-recyclable footage.

There was also a third soul inside of him.

When I was small, I looked up at my daddy and saw everything I wanted to be and everything I was afraid of. Back then I couldn't hold all the parts of him in the palms of my tiny hands, so I had to choose, and I did. His presence became a blanket of safety over hearts that were shivering from neglect. When he laughed I let his laugh swallow me up.

I asked him once, looking him in the eyes, to explain the meaning of my middle name,

"Time of trouble," he responded, his laugh coming out in a small huff.

I scrunched up my face and scoffed. He didn't elaborate, but I didn't care. When he was there he swallowed up all that trouble and all the demons went limping off, temporarily, into damp corners.

At night, I'd close my eyes and the different parts of him would go to war with each other for my affection. I'd wonder what Mum felt when the palm of his large hands connected with the delicate surface of her face. I'd wonder how the same hands that held me affectionately could cause her skin to bruise and swell. I wondered and wondered and wondered. I wanted someone to tell me which version of him was the real one. Or maybe I didn't really want to know. My dad was a politician by day, and at night he kept campaigning inside my head, making promises to amend the constitution of our home. My mom's cheek, her screams and sobs — convincing forms of propaganda, all the reasons not to trust him; but always, I'd give him my vote. I told you he was persuasive. It was always a selfish choice in the end, a choice made out of the need to survive. I memorized the sound of his feet coming up the front steps of our house, the soft patter of his dark brown wing tip oxfords. I memorized the sound of his feet leaving in the mornings, sometimes for days at a time. All I wanted was to petition the second soul to stay forever. But I was never as convincing as he was.

Conceivably you are wondering how I could have loved a man who beat my mother as I watched from the sidelines, my delicate voice pleading for him to stop. How I still leaped into his arms when I heard his keys vibrate against the metal of the deadbolt. I understand.

Let me explain: there was a certain order, a hierarchy that could not be challenged. My mother belonged to my father, and we belonged to my mother. Those were the rules. And when my daddy was there, my mother was so preoccupied with her own fear it created a little pothole in time, allowing us to emerge from the shadows and breathe. I am part monster myself, it seems, because when the small sliver of space appeared, I could not waste it by becoming overly sympathetic to her experience of pain. It is not something I am proud of, but at the time it was the only sensible choice. The apple doesn't fall far from the tree and all that.

There was a lot about Mum that I respected. I can finally look backward and acknowledge her strength and courage. After school I'd sometimes do my homework on the floor of her office. I looked up and watched her assert herself as a competent, confident woman, a woman capable of holding her own in a realm dominated by men. She weathered the unpredictable zigzags of my father's political involvement like a champion, adapting and shifting to fit in neatly beside him as he fine tuned his political agenda. It sowed a seed of potential inside of me. She was a pioneer, a fighter, a shining example of silent endurance. I now realize that sometimes, in order to survive, you have to trade in your softness and your heart, you have to let yourself go numb and cold; but, at the time I resented how she never seemed to break character, how her strength rendered her almost robotic. Don't misunderstand me, she was beautiful and charming, especially when the world was watching. When everyone knows your name, it is important to make an impression. And she did. She threw the most amazing parties. Everyone marveled at her colorful dresses, the bold prints of her chitenge popping vibrantly off her skin. She instructed every worker with clarity and precision leaving a presentation of food and drink that everyone arrived and praised her for. I marveled too, because for parties she metamorphosed into some radiant stranger.

And I didn't question it, I just soaked it in, and let her pretend to be the mother I had waited longingly for. I just asked for two slices of chocolate cake and ate every morsel of both, while she laughed warmly at how adorable I was. I ignored that telling flicker of disgust in her eyes that everyone else failed to notice. She played the role of politician's wife immaculately. I envied the version of her that the rest of the world got to have. As I watched the cars drive away one by one, I would feel my heart start knocking about wildly. I'd tilt my body toward her, smiling slightly just in case that stranger had decided to stay. But she was gone.

I want to tell you about the things that went on when the parties were over. I want to tell you so that we can understand each other. But it is like having a camera shoved up against and inside your most private parts, and I admit a reluctance to expose myself in such a manner.

I KNOW SO little about how my parents met. It is a narrative I have often wished someone would fill in for me. As an adult, great aunt told me that when they met, their love and commitment to one another left everyone nursing pangs of envy. My dad had, supposedly, wooed my mom with such grand romance, even an independent spirit such as herself could not resist him. Together they had an unmatchable strength. He the sort of man that made space for her opinions and challenge, from matters of law to matters of spirituality. She unafraid to speak for herself and yet soft enough to defer to him when it made sense. I never knew the people great aunt described, the tenor of her voice lifting slightly as she recalled the early days with fondness. She had raised my mom, and so when daddy came around, she had been proud to invite him into the family. As she told the story, I found my lips turning up in a slight smile, my heart aching and wondering what it would have been like to be parented by the people she described. I ruminated silently about what it was that had fragmented their love. What I witnessed of their relationship felt tumultuous and volatile. When there was conflict it roared to life and clawed our paper perfection to shreds, leaving every room awash in unease. When there was passion those sobs turned to sighs and moans in the middle of the night. This was the fractured reality of love laid as a foundation inside of me. Everywhere I turned, the same hands that stroked in affection wounded in rage. I couldn't make sense of it. Life was like an unsolvable equation. In mathematics variables remain constant so that you can, eventually, find a solution to the problem, but as a child the solution was elusive, the variables constantly shape shifting from safe to unsafe without warning. It was like that for my parents' relationship and the same was true for my relationship with Mum. She would become enraged if we didn't hug her the way we hugged Daddy or would become jealous if we were affectionate with other family members or friends. And so in absolute terror I would shuffle my feet nearer to her and put my arms around her waist, only to be pinched and poked, beaten and criticized. I had a house full of toys but if I played with them too long, I was lazy, not long enough and I was ungrateful. I just wanted someone to tell me what I should and shouldn't do. I wanted someone to paint in bright red all the places that I wasn't allowed to step. I wanted to know when to laugh and when to stop laughing. That perfect amount of distance to walk beside her so I wasn't too close and I wasn't too far away. I wanted someone to give me a list of acceptable responses and another of appropriate things to talk casually about with someone who terrifies you. I felt ashamed that I could not seem to master this. I wanted to please her. I desperately wanted to learn the guidelines of my mother's emotions, perhaps earn her affection as a reward, but they were always changing. It created a fear so rich in me, I could close my eyes and hear it in there, cackling away.

This is the part of abuse people don't want to talk about. People hear that word and imagine bumps and bruises, cuts, scars, blood. And trust me, those things were present in abundance — but it's the other things. That constant mental torture that is invisible to the naked eye; the way your entire body is persistently on high alert, or the way nothing surprises you and yet everything surprises you. It's the living every moment trying to avoid landmines, the sigh you breath when you've fooled yourself into believing that you have finally learned the rules to keep you safe, only to discover that new landmines are being buried every minute and that there isn't any safe place to step. Eventually and in the end, there is only one rule that seemed to matter: it is not safe to feel safe.

FLATLINE

Your love is a minefield
     One misstep, a frightened flinch and
     Brain plays bumper cars with skull
     Blindly clutching
     Cradling an arm lost in the blast
     Blood splattering
     like ruby fireworks
     You learn the rules by breaking them
     If you want to survive dance inside
     Shape shifting invisible lines

Your love is a maze
     Every day a new riddle
     Your breath, a clue - your eyes,
     The twitch in your lip
     A warped lesson in hypervigilance
     Sleep with knees pressed into the grass
     One eye hanging open
     Teeth still rattling from the explosion that
     emptied her tiny eye sockets
     Hardened the other's heart

Your love is thief
     an uninvited wisp of cold air
     On the underside of my left breast
     Your hands making themselves at home
     Bandits of hope
     Vultures licking their lips at the sight
     Of weakness rendering wounds
     Dismantled the outside with ease
     Now plunder the insides
     Pupils dilated with greed

Your love is a promise
    Thumb pressed lazily over the detonator
    Bombs strapped to my back
    A whisper, a challenge, an invitation
    To strive for the other side
    Amble cautiously toward freedom
    All the while knowing
    Even if you arrive intact
    One firm press of the thumb and
    Flatline

I want to say I relished the days that they were affectionate with each other. My sisters and I would put our hands over our eyes in embarrassment as they kissed and embraced without restraint, my mother laughing at some secret words my father had laced into her ears. We would sit around the table in our kitchen and eat dinner as a paper family. I'd laugh because it was expected, all the while pressing my gnawed fingernails into the skin of my thigh, waiting just in case things changed unexpectedly. On those days, they would usher us into bed early. I'd lie there with my back pressed into the mattress, eyes staring up at the ceiling and listen to my mom moaning passionately. I wanted to know if her moans were part of the pretending we were doing, or whether she really knew how to let herself be loved and caressed by the same man who, only days before, had marked her pristine skin. I want to tell you that I relished those days, but I don't want to play paper pretend with you. Those days when my parents loved each other were the hardest days. One foolish part of my insides would peak its head out and look on with crossed fingers, hoping that this time their love would stick. But it never did stick and the penalty for disrupted love always fell on us girls to pay. I'd lie there with my eyes open, listening to the chorus of passion knowing that, in a few days, when they no longer loved each other, I would, perhaps, be forced to sleep beside my mother in the spare bedroom.

Love itself was a landmine, it seemed.

FOR A LONG TIME I did not know what to call the ways the fingers moved against me in the middle of the night. I did not know what to call it when you have to lie still and let yourself be explored in that way. I did not know what to call the way the pain causes your soul to reluctantly dislocate from your body and float above, watching and mourning the parts of you that are dying before its very eyes. I didn't want my soul to watch but it could not look away. I did not want my body to respond, did not want to feel parts of myself wake up while others were dying, suffocated underneath the unwelcome gravity of violation. I trembled from the shame, my soul looking down at my body in disgust, my body glancing away in remorse. Those moments were the forceful dismemberment of my wholeness. Do you know what it is like to hate yourself for a response you can't control? I wanted to disappear. I wanted to scream. I wanted to strangle myself and die.

Did you ever notice that there is only a very slight difference between the words 'rapture' and 'rupture'? That is what you might imagine seeing here, that very slight difference materialized. Two bodies, both breathing heavily, both eyes shut, one sighing in rapture, one holding back the screams caused by the weight of rupture.

I watched the door and listened while the blood rushed in rivers through my ears. I prayed through gritted teeth for an interruption. I tasted the tears sliding down my cheeks. I held my breath and waited for someone to come home, metal against the deadbolt, explode into the dark bedroom, grab that slender throat and shake it until the teeth fell out. I watched and watched.

But no one ever came.

In that house on the hill your body becomes currency, an automated teller machine. Your body is everything but in order to be everything, it must first become nothing, do you understand what I am saying?

I WAS THERE BUT THE WORDS WEREN'T WITH ME

I was there but the words weren't with me
    left me abandoned
    bolted down in the tidal wave of pure sensation
    frozen and overcome
    awash in currents of confusion
    the impact of shock on the mind
    I was there but my voice wasn't with me
    departed silently and without warning
    rendering me aphasic
    catatonic
    a prisoner of touch
    I should have screamed
    or pleaded
    I should have — something
    I was there and my body was with me
    with me but not mine
    with me but yours
    with me but imprisoned
    the tenor of your voice stunning me into
    paralyzed compliance
    like a tranquilizer
    like a gun against the soft part of my skull
    yet still moving against your secret places
    under selfish instruction
    I should have clawed
    Rebelled against this forced act of being
    Reborn // the act of being regenerated, created again
    made new as you pushed yourself on me
    gyrating your hips, pushed into me
    your insides contracting
    mine alive with hidden tremors
    a sigh - a release
    rebirthed a shadow of former things

fractured, I am
there but the words aren't with me
caught in a loop of unannounced sensation
those broad arms of fear
dragging me backward and under and
into the tidal wave of pure
You
I should scream
I should claw
I should
Something

When we weren't in school we spent our days taking French lessons, or piano lessons or traveling as a family. Great Aunt always describes us as spoiled, and we were in many ways spoiled. We got to have experiences she often said she had never gotten to have, even as an adult. When Mum insisted that we take piano lessons, I was initially excited for a reason to spend more time away from home. I liked the independence I felt when our driver dropped big sister and I off, announcing that he would return within two hours, at the end of both of our lessons. Big sister would go first while I occupied myself drawing with sticks in the dirt outside the little house where we practiced. I'd skip and sing to myself and listen to the notes coming through the window shakily. When it was my turn I passed the crooked drawing stick off to big sister. I straightened my dress and dusted off my shoes and entered the small square house. I waited as the teacher pulled the piano stool back and invited me to sit comfortably in the center. In these memories the teacher had the sort of presence that filled up the entire room, the entire house, perhaps. He stood very straight, his shoulders set back and his head held high. Something about him intimidated me. But then again, I was characteristically quite wary of adults in general. I had the feeling that I did not want to embarrass myself in front of him so I worked hard to master the skills that he demonstrated. I did my best to understand how the little circles and lines in the floppy book in front of me corresponded with the places my fingers were meant to bare down on the piano keys. I learned Middle C as the grounding place, a place to return to when my fingers got lost or rebelliously traveled too far down the shiny white rectangles. He clapped when I did things well, and when I didn't he squeezed his hand against my shoulder to invite me to start again. It did not hurt but it got my attention. I shook my head in frustration, sighed and began again. It was good. Boring, but good. Week after week I progressed steadily. My scales floated around the room in a less choppy manner and after a while the notes on the page turned into familiar friends I did not have to squint so hard to recognize.

It was after I had played through a longer piece in its entirety for the first time that my ears twitched, expecting to hear the familiar clapping of the teacher's broad hands as I pressed down on the last notes. But instead of those broad hands meeting each other in the air, I found them reaching around me from behind, at first just a tight hug. It shocked and confused me but it was just a brief embrace so I left it. After that his hands never met each other in midair but instead, like snakes slipped around my waist as he squatted down behind me, those dry hands sneaking their way down the front of my shirt as I played. I found it hard to breathe with his hand against the phantom of my left breast or against the hidden flesh of my inner thigh and his breath leaving moisture on my earlobe.

I was there but the words weren't with me.

———

A FEW TIMES A YEAR, the mundane shuffling of life paused to make room for us to travel as a family. Daddy would lock up his papers and store away his briefcase for a time. He traded in his three piece suits and leather shoes for shorts and lightweight button down shirts and joined us as we explored the neighboring countries or flew across the ocean to wander around Europe for a while. We buckled ourselves up in spacious business class seats and when we arrived at our destination, stayed at posh hotels where people brought us our breakfast on trays while we stayed overlong in bed. We walked through new cities, our feet adjusting to the unevenness of cobblestone or our eyes marveling at the big red busses sliding across the streets, daddy and Mum filling our ears with history. We flew to England to visit mum's childhood friend. Her accent sounded like poetry, like the pages of a book you never wanted to end. I loved the other worldliness of the place. I loved how imposing the buildings felt, the way Big Ben kept watch over residents and tourists, alike. I wanted to bury myself inside the slight and constant chill in the air. We'd walk and walk and walk, taking in sights that added new layers of dimension and depth to my imagination. It was as we stood in front of Buckingham Palace that I promised myself I would make this place my home someday. One day I would get on an airplane all by myself, and I would never come back. The prospect excited me. I wanted to see the whole world, but I wanted to live inside a flat with a red door in the middle of London. I wanted to sip my tea while I read books beside a window that looked out over the dreary and grey skies. On other trips we bopped up and down as safari drivers pointed out all the animals, instructing us to sit still and silent as we took in the stretching jaws of lions and snapped pictures of elephants on our disposable cameras. We walked through nature, my small hand held tightly in my daddy's oversized one until we stood at the edge of plunging waterfalls. The vastness suited my daddy. We'd swim in the crisp clear water, our voices echoing off boulders large enough to swallow us whole. It sounds like a dream, doesn't it? And it was. When he was there, life seemed exactly like a dream. It was as if time was frozen and we stepped into a moment in which happiness was more than fleeting paper; as if I was experiencing the great love story that drew these two beings together to begin with, and in that story there was enough love to go around. I never wanted it to end.

It was at the tail-end of one of these excursions that baby sister was born. Mum was robust with the movement of her third girl inside her belly, straining constantly as we ran along the shorelines of Cape Town. All that straining sent her into an early labor and right there in the middle of our vacation and baby sister greeted the world with eyes that have remained vibrant until this day. She was small and sweet and as her small hand made a fist around my fingers, I pitied her. I imagined shoving her back inside of Mum where she was, undoubtedly safer. I imagined carrying her off and raising her myself. Her birth shook my insides violently. It made me question with even more fervor the disconnection between Mum and me. As she cradled baby sister inside of her arms, I wondered if it had started out like this for me. I wanted to ask her. I wanted to strip myself naked and make myself a small ball in her arms; to start again. Shortly after big sister had to have her tonsils removed. I watched Mum attend to her with affection, bringing her popsicles to suck on as she recovered. I was jealous. I was tempted to ask the doctor to remove my tonsils too, just so that I could earn a moment of tender attention.

After baby sister was born, Great Aunt would sometimes tell me, "You were born in the middle to hold both of your sisters up."

She said it even when we were all grown up. By that time my arms were getting tired, and I wondered silently to myself if anyone was ever going to hold me up for a change.

HOPE

Hope is sacred aliveness
   A vulnerable sprout splitting musky earth
   And I — it's unskilled gardener
   Black thumbed and over eager
   Meticulous, assiduous — an erratic pendulum, too
   swaying between catatonic fear and
   unconstrained glee

"How do I keep it alive?"
   sails my voice into the waiting ether, with a wobble,
   as if dizzy, as if half drunk with fear
   while my brows furrow and my timid hands tremble

"Sing it a song," replies the wind
   while her wispy fingers reach to stroke my face —
   an attempt to soften the worry etched into the lines there

— —

I buried my dreams alive so that she would no longer have
   the pleasure of doing so
   Buried them alive to save time and labor
   Walked myself to the shallow grave
   Bent scuffed knees to soft earth and
   Inside I laid them gently

Here they lie
   Here they lie

Sprinkled soft earth against their still beating hearts
   Leaked tears to fall and water what could never be
   Leaked tears to honor what I believed

would never become
Leaked tears to honor the failure to thrive
Sang a crooked lullaby
while I left a small rock as a crude tombstone
Never to be forgotten

Here they lie

Who knew hope could bloom from the seeds of
buried dreams?
Could nudge its way to the surface and
cut a line through hardened earth to strain toward the light
Who knew hope could bloom from the seeds of
buried dreams?
Could defy the odds and insist with unyielding defiance
to bring life to a place made barren by grief
and by trauma
sprout to teach an unskilled gardener
that though only now felt between the pads of fingers
though only now seen as green life above the surface
of seemingly dead earth —
hope has been a thriving system of tangled roots
always thriving, always surviving,
refusing entirely to be killed off and
snuffed out

Who knew hope could bloom for the seeds of
buried dreams?
Shake them loose from their slumber
Bloom to exhume and offer a rebirth or
a resurrection, maybe

———————————————————————

Hope is a sacred aliveness
    A stunningly resilient sprout splitting musky earth
    And I — its unskilled gardener

At least twice a year we made visits to see extended family in a city a few hours outside of where we lived. Daddy did not come on those trips, but there were enough watching eyes to insulate mom's temper — but not always. These people raised her. They knew all about her temper and how she did not enjoy being challenged, especially over matters, such as us, that did not concern them.

I loved it there, especially when Mum dropped us off for weeks at a time and returned home. On the night before I knew we would be going, my whole body would be shaking with anticipation, making it difficult to sleep. When it was time to leave and return home, I pulled at my great aunt and asked her if I could stay. I cried loudly and buried my face into the floor. In later years, she told me it had always made her heart squeeze in agony. She said she wished she could have let me stay, though she did not understand why I was so desperate to be away from Mum; even she understood her limits.

In K-town, we spent our days walking up and down the city roads, stopping for popsicles, sticking our heads into neighbors' homes, and sitting outside on the small screened in porch swatting at the flies that had managed to sneak in. We ate mangoes everyday. We sent the taller men out to reach them for us or bravely used our bare feet to try and anchor ourselves as we tried to shimmy up on our own. I would bite straight through the skin of the ripe ones; that fleshy pulp dripped down my hands and stained my shirt. I sliced the immature green ones and sprinkled salt on their insides.

We went to the pool hall down the road and spent our crinkled money on arcade games. I had my first drink in that pool hall. It happened when I was eleven. My big sister had been allowed to go out for New Years Eve the year before while I was required to stay back. I spent the evening stubbornly sulking, resenting being considered one of the babies. I declined the vanilla ice cream that was offered to soften the blow. I was not a baby, I insisted. And so the following year, they did not argue with me, when I, at the ripe age of eleven, declared myself old and mature enough to spend the evening out with the older girls. We met our older female cousin and her friends in that smoky pool hall. The lights were dim and the music was loud. It looked different in the night time than it did in the day, no longer disguised underneath a veil of innocence. The older men smoked cigarettes and emptied glasses of liquor into their mouths. I sat in one of their laps, shifting around anxiously and sipped a Jack and Coke. It didn't taste particularly good, but after a while, the burning wore off. I remember that I could not sit still and that the furniture seemed to have come alive. I did not particularly enjoy the feeling, but I certainly was not about to make a fuss.

K-town was full of second cousins and their children. Although to be clear, second cousins are not a thing where I come from; second cousins are aunts and their children are your cousins, and everyone else is still a version of family. They were loud, shuffling in and out of their parents' house, that house the center of life. They screamed lengthy stories, their voices competing for space. I giggled at their antics, the way they bickered, gap-toothed mouths open wide, about nothing and nonsense. At night, Great Uncle would come home after a long day of work. As soon as he opened the door, a sense of peace settled over the house. The bickering stopped and everyone wound down until the pulse of the house evened into something soft and steady. Us kids would run and stand in front of Great Uncle, smiling our best smiles and crossing our fingers behind our backs that he would choose us. When he pointed his finger in my direction, I smiled proudly at my cousins and sisters. I'd kneel in front of him and take his shoes off before innocently tickling the bottom of his broad feet. His whole body would vibrate with laughter until he picked me up and tickled my side until I was laughing with tears coming out of my eyelids. It was a silly ritual of his, but his laughter felt intoxicating and soothing. Even from the sidelines, on those days I was not chosen, I simply could not resist being drawn into it, my own body shaking with joy as if his long fingers were digging into my armpit playfully.

I adored all of my aunts, but I loved one in particular; her demeanor was more quiet and overall warmer. I suppose she felt kindred to me in that way. I did not tell her my secrets, but still, she exuded safety and peace. She asked me to be the flower girl in her wedding, and I was elated to be the one chosen. She curled my hair and tied a ribbon through the ends; for once I felt like I was the beautiful one, even though the story I heard afterward was about the way the dress I'd worn had to be let out to accomodate my pudgy belly. At her reception, we ate pieces of cake and danced for hours. I loved the man she was marrying. He was strong but gentle. In truth, I wanted him for myself. At the end, as the bride and groom were about to leave for their honeymoon, I sat down at her feet in a pile of tears. I had not realized that the night would end with them leaving. She picked me up in her wide arms, looked at my eyes and laughed, vowing that they would be back in a week. Departures were always traumatic for me. Life felt so terribly fickle. I could never trust whether safe people would be coming back or if they would be gone for good.

I often wondered why we did not just move to K-town. Mum seemed happier there. Perhaps happier is a stretch, but at the very least she did not seem as perpetually vexed. She laughed more, and it seemed that it actually reached the center of her eyes. When we were there, I seemed to catch glimpses of what she might have been like as a child, and maybe even a bit after that. There, she had a place in the jovial mayhem at the house. Her cousins looked to her to take their side in meaningless debates, and she would just shake her head and use her fat tongue to tsk, tsk at them. They would roll their eyes and shake their heads back as if used to her constant diplomacy in their dramas. My cousins and I amped up our own drama to match that of the adults. We took turns sprinting to this auntie or that uncle tattle tailing on one another, one story not yet finished before another was beginning. In these matters, I often played Mum's role. I did not break confidence, and I did not agree or disagree. The cousins would sigh at me in exasperation, fed up with my unwillingness to corroborate their stories. I did not budge. It gave me a power I did not want to part with so easily.

LINEAGE

I am my mother's past
    outfitted by those unspoken transgressions
    the chafing, untrimmed talons of unspent grief
    holding her heart like fresh plucked wildflowers.

When I was eight years old, my parents made the decision to send big sister and I to boarding school in South Africa. Baby sister was just two years old at the time, and not old enough to join us. At first it was scary, flying to another country, two unaccompanied minors being toted around by whatever air hostess was kind enough to assist us. There hadn't been a discussion about boarding school. No one bothered to explain why we were going or how long we would be staying. I was, admittedly, terrified, but big sister was in the seat beside me so I comforted myself by reaching over and squeezing her fingers in mine.

The school was large, the boarding campus housed inside two tall iron gates with the school crest branded in the middle. Driving up I wasn't sure if the gate was meant to keep the students in or the rest of the world out, but I guess it served a dual purpose. As I dragged my suitcase into the dormitory, I quickly realized I was the smallest of the girls living at the school. The others did not hesitate to make sure I was aware of this fact. On my first day there one of the older girls asked me what time it was. I told her,

"Five thirty five."

"Five twenty five?" she asked me. I could already tell this was going sideways, for some reason I could not identify.

"No, five thirty five," I said again. She shook her head and ran back to the dorm to check the time for herself. She came back and announced that it was "twenty five to six," and the rest of the girls laughed at my supposed inability to tell the time. I swallowed back my frustration.

It did not take long for me to realize the small paradise I had stumbled upon. At night one girl would whimper and wail in her twin bed, calling out for her mother, kept awake by the severest form of home sickness I had ever witnessed. I could not relate. For me, it was not difficult to adjust to the freedom. I felt euphoric and invincible. The knowledge that my mother was an entire plane ride away felt like a surge of power. I was not accustomed to sleeping so soundly through the night. I was not accustomed to the silliness of living in a big room full of girls, climbing over and into each others beds to tell secrets and stories. We were in trouble every night, our dorm mother poking her head into the darkness to scold us and threaten us with study hall the next day. Perhaps I should have educated her on what it takes to frighten a child into submission.

On the weekend we would take outings to the shopping mall. We'd watch movies and shovel pieces of chocolate into our mouths. We'd sneak out and spend our money on boxes of spicy chips, eating them in a circle on the bathroom floor. Every day we'd ride the bus back to the dorms from the primary school campus, throw our shoes off before the bus came to a halt, and take off as soon as the door opened. We'd sprint, our bodies shaking with giggles, all the way to the common area so we could catch the end of Days of Our Lives before changing for dinner. It was as if a whole world had been opened up to me. A world in which believing that you could be the next Spice Girl was permissible. A world in which there was space to fall in love with older boys who didn't know you existed. Do you know what it is like to laugh without restraint? It is its own form of magic. I still remember the first time I watched the older boys play rugby, their tiny shorts revealing muscular quadriceps. I felt my cheeks get hot and hid my face behind big sister's shoulder.

It seemed we were always playing, always laughing, inviting each other into worlds we had created in our minds. We wrote plays and performed them for our teachers, pulled out all our leisure clothes and styled each other then walked through the rows of study hall, our hips swaying to Santana's Maria Maria as we embodied high fashion models. We never talked about where we had come from. I never told the girls that I was afraid to go home, because for these isolated moments in time, fear was not a reality, and home seemed worlds away.

For the primary schoolers, the school was separated into two parts, the day school a few miles down the road, where the rickety bus deposited us every morning to take our courses, and the actual boarding campus, which was also where the secondary students completed their studies. Most of the boarding students were black like me, although the list of countries they all called home were vast. I picked up Portuguese words from my sister's first boyfriend from Mozambique, and learned French songs from my best friends from Congo. When we were cross at one another, we'd link arms with the people who spoke the same language as us and tell secrets no one else could interpret.

The day school brought with it an additional layer of diversity. Many of the children, whose parents drove them to school, were white. During the day, they sometimes tilted their noses up at the darker skinned kids. The black children did it too, don't get me wrong. At home my family had friends who were white. When white people did things that were annoying I often heard my mom suck air in through her teeth and whisper something about the Mzungu's. I didn't pay much attention to whether it was meant in a derogatory way, but other than that word, I never heard her speak ill of another race. South Africa, in that way was different than what I was used to, the country still trying to shake off the cloak of apartheid that had sat like a brick upon its shoulders for too long. We'd watch Sarafina! in history class, learning about the historical significance of Nelson Mandela being the president at the time. The whole country was straining against old chains of thinking and hustling toward a future that, hopefully, waved a banner of equality. I could relate to that struggle, my own insides constantly stretching toward a freedom and peace it had been pining for.

IT DID NOT OCCUR to me to think about life at home while I was away at school. Perhaps for once I just wanted to let myself stand fully in one place. I liked the feeling of uniformity that possessed my insides, as if for once I did not have to be a split screen.

For the first term, I made the mistake of forgetting my mother entirely. I lost myself in swim team and netball and boys so completely that it wasn't until my school teacher handed me my report card before our first break that I was forced to remember. I sat in my seat on the airplane sweating, my poor marks in Afrikaans calling out to me from the overhead compartment. I wanted to push the button above me and ask the flight attendant to let me borrow the oxygen mask to manage my internal emergency. I wanted to find the nearest exit and throw myself out the window and land with my feet firmly planted in Pretoria. I was having trouble managing the fear. I had gotten out of the habit of hypervigilance. I had less than a two hour flight to remember.

I looked for my dad's car as we arrived at the house. Unsurprisingly it was not there. Report card in hand we entered the house. I did not let myself imagine what it might feel like for her to run over and embrace me, eyes wet with how much she missed us. I just wrapped my fist around my grades and extended them out toward her.

It was then that she pulled a dinner plate out of the cabinet and slammed it down over my head. My knees betrayed me and I buckled down to the floor, broken pieces sticking out of my curly hair. I didn't make a sound, terrified I would provoke her further. I wanted to look up at her and see if any sign of love would flicker across her face, to know if she was moved by my pain. I didn't have time to find out because it was then that she pulled a wooden cooking spoon out of the drawer, left of the stove. She played that spoon against my body like it was a drum. I did not recognize the song. I wish I knew how to tell you how it feels to have your body turned into an instrument. I wish I could tell you what it takes to stifle the screams and the cries because you know, you *know* how much she hates it when you whimper. It is as if you yourself become a split screen, body and soul fractured, waiting and waiting and waiting until, finally, with a snap of the spoon the song finally ends.

So you will no doubt understand why it was always a relief when, on half term breaks from school, Mum and Daddy decided not to fly us home. They would instead send us to stay with a family friend for the week and a half before classes resumed. He would pick us up in his aging car and throw his arms around us as if we were well acquainted. I would shiver as he sucked on my neck as he said hello, his hot breath lingering like a cloud even after he had released me. It seemed we were always choosing between the lessor of two horrors. I hated the way his hands seemed to graze me in places I did not give him permission to touch and the way his tongue seemed to sneak its way onto my skin. I didn't dare complain. It wasn't worth it. And frankly, in the grand scheme of things, these seemed like minor inconveniences that I could weather better than the alternative. He worked during the day and while he was away, big sister and I had his apartment to ourselves. He'd stock the shelves with Pringles and Aero chocolate bars and leave money on the kitchen counter for us to order pizza or chicken wings. We spent the week between terms filling our bellies and watching R rated movies on his small television. In the evening, right before dinnertime, I'd find my school calendar and add one more big "X" in gel pen, one more day closer to when we could return to school.

It was during a lengthier break, in the unwelcome space between second and third term, that we witnessed the worst and most violent altercation between Mum and daddy. We always seemed to enter the story in the middle, right at the climax, so forgive me, because I cannot tell you what came before. I can hardly tell you what came after. I was sucking my thumb while sitting on the armchair of our couch. I was watching television, let's say Rugrats. Big sister and I were teasing baby sister for the way she whined and tattled, a little bully like Angelica Pickles. I was on the inhale of a big laugh when I first heard the china land on the kitchen floor. The laugh never came out.

At the threshold of the kitchen I watched Mum leap atop daddy's back, banging her fists at his big head. He shifted her around with ease, one arm catching in her hair, the other rearing back before connecting with her jaw. I pleaded for him to stop, praying that he would recognize my voice and that the second soul would take hold of him again. I screamed his name louder. Her thighs rippled as she landed on the floor. I knew what it felt like to be left in pain on that very floor and I wanted to run to her. But I was frozen. It did not stop until large arms were pulling us backwards and away from the door, our cook perhaps, or the driver. It did not stop until we had been sitting with the door to the living room pressed shut, rocking our bodies back and forth to soothe the grief. It did not stop until the front door slammed shut with a bang, the familiar sound of keys scraping against the deadbolt.

It did not take long after daddy left before Mum herself dressed, summoned the driver and sped off. We sat for hours waiting. It is remarkable the stories your mind can create in the unsteady silence of waiting. I was of course used to Daddy's unexplained departures, but Mum? It was not like her to walk out before rattling off a reason and a few expectations to fill the time that she was gone. I would not call what I felt "missing her," but I did wonder what it meant and what it could mean that both of them had taken off like that, leaving us in stunned silence in the center of the living room.

Mum, as it turned out, had driven herself to the police station to file an assault charge against the third soul living inside my daddy. She returned later with her face mottled and swollen. My instincts took over and when I saw her, I let my small hand glide against her cheek. For some reason she let me. That, perhaps, was more shocking than the color her cheek was turning, that purple-grey hue staring at me and screaming, "look at what your daddy can do." I ignored it almost entirely. It is unfair that a small child should have to have such thoughts living inside her head, don't you agree? Especially when she has been trying to convince herself all afternoon that it had not truly been her daddy she had seen in the kitchen that afternoon.

By the time the break ended, Mum had packed us girls up and found us an apartment to live in, separate from daddy.

For a while this move away from him felt almost inconsequential. It was not like Daddy had been making a habit of hanging around for long stretches of time before this. He always appeared with his broad smile, stuffing a few bills into our waiting palms, which we quickly squandered on cheap jewelry in the marketplace nestled between him and our new home. Of course when we first stepped foot into the new dimly lit two bedroom condo, I was welcomed with the onset of my own secret anxiety, not visible to the naked eye. I was aware that he did not possess a key to this new place, that here it would not be logical to wait for the scrape of metal fitting into the nooks of the deadbolt. I was aware, but as I said, for a time it was inconsequential. I nursed my fear on the hope of South Africa, like a pacifier fitted into the waiting mouth of a child, and at first it was enough. The break ended and big sister and I boarded the plane as usual. The wheels touched down and we went back to life as normal. We tucked that new condo, with its grey walls and insufficient lighting into our empty luggage and chucked it into the storage closet and forgot it entirely. Well almost entirely. That term our dorm mother and her husband argued fiercely in the middle of the night. One morning, as she roused us from sleep, I noticed the way her cheek was stained purple blue. I wanted to apologize to her; some of the bad had snuck out of my suitcase and into her home, it seemed.

It is interesting, isn't it, how pieces of your life may be taking shape at times entirely without your knowledge? How while you are having a water fight in the middle of the bathroom with your friends, or scrunching your nose up at the strawberry yogurt being served for breakfast, the police could be driving to your farm house and banging on the door, presenting your daddy with a warrant for his arrest, or pushing him roughly into the dark corners of a prison cell. And this is exactly how it was. When we packed our bags at the end of third term and when the driver picked us up on the other side, the two separate pieces of our lives shook hands in greeting, the one side looking at the other as if to say,

"We have a lot of catching up to do."

When big sister and I were first told that daddy was recently imprisoned, I assumed it was because of the way he had used his hands against Mum's body before we went back to school. I confess I am not certain who eventually relayed the events of the last two weeks to us. They did their best but the narrative was difficult to follow. I did not, at the time, understand words like "coup" or "treason" and the explanations being rattled off did little to clarify the terms. All I managed to piece together was that daddy was now behind bars, that this had something to do with his political involvement and that the accusations were severe. It all seemed so much bigger than me, so much bigger than my small frame knew what to do with, like a made up story and not my own life. I wanted to skip to the last page and get to the ending already. You can relate, I am sure.

It was not until our first visit to the prison that I understood the fullness of what was happening. Mum made us dress in our best clothes, those itchy Sunday dresses that left me in a constant state of discomfort. She pulled our hair into buns and adorned our heads with bows. I didn't understand what all the fuss was about, but as we pulled up to the prison gates and saw the reporters, I quickly realized, that even here, the world was watching. We parked the car and walked across the muddy road, careful not to sully our polished shoes. Mum, the ever devoted public wife, brought with her parcels of daddy's favorite food and some of his clothes. She told us firmly that we were to be on our best behavior and that we should avoid asking questions. I knew what she meant: when we saw daddy, we had to just pretend he was not sitting across from us with shackles on his ankles.

Inside, the air felt coated in sorrow, those unseen echoes of tears floated into me through my ear canals and resurrected a twin sorrow inside me. The smell of unshowered bodies intermingled with whatever food the prisoners were served to create a concoction that made my stomach turn over. I wanted to wretch into a vacant corner, but I knew it was not an option. We walked steadily onward, as the heavy boots of the guards bounced off the walls and their guns flapped against their sides in warning. I wanted to turn around and run out for a breath of air, free of prison musk and terror.

We sat around the rectangular table in a small meeting room while one guard excused himself to go and retrieve daddy. My heart was pounding frantically. I felt excited to see him but excitement did not seem an appropriate emotion in a setting such as this one. We heard him before we saw him, his ankle chains dragging against the concrete floor. The heavy door creaked open and his body was shoved in. I looked up at him and it was like suddenly everything was happening in slow motion. I wanted to jump up and run to him, but as I took in his appearance, the shock landed inside my stomach like a cinderblock and I could not seem to move. I could not understand how this was the same man I had seen a few months prior. His white shirt danced around his withering frame, and bags hung limply underneath his eyes. He smiled as he looked at us but it was not a real smile. It was the biggest pretend smile I had seen yet. Mum shoved us firmly toward him and I finally moved to wrap my arms around his waist. For the first time in my life, his stomach did not feel like a pillow as I pressed my head into it. It was difficult not to cry. No, it was difficult not to come undone entirely. He may as well have been standing there naked in front of me, this superhuman stripped of all his power; just a man. I looked up at the guards with their bulky guns and I wanted to ask them what they had done to my daddy. I wanted them to go back out and return with the rest of him. The man I knew did not belong in a place like this, the whole situation felt mismatched.

We sat at that table, my hand resting atop his. He kept smiling while asking us about school and about the marks on our report cards. On the outside we laughed about nonsense in our paper way, the guards watching us out of the corner of their eyes. On the inside the smell of the food we'd brought was making me nauseous. The heaviness of everything we were not acknowledging was sitting inside my chest and all the questions were bouncing around inside my head like a rubber ball. I was not accustomed to my daddy smelling foul or seeing his bare feet exposed and dirty. I looked at him with a smile plastered on my face and fear sitting inside my big brown eyes. Perhaps he could see because he gave me a small wink. It did nothing to settle me down.

We passed the remaining weeks of that Christmas break making visits to the prison. We did not move back to the farm, as I hoped. It was like a double loss, being away from daddy and being away from home. We kept bringing food to the doors of the prison, but daddy's size, I noticed, was not improving. The life seemed to be leaking out of his skin, and he looked grey and sallow. The smile he continued to flash at us made me feel angry and helpless. Every night I fell asleep with horrific stories playing out inside my mind. No one was talking to us about what was happening and my mind was grappling to make meaning out of the pieces. I didn't know if daddy would ever come home. I didn't know whether he was eating, and if he wasn't, I wondered how long the human body can survive without food. I didn't even know why he was in the prison, and I certainly did not want to think about what would happen if he was truly guilty of what he was being accused of. As Christmas inched closer, I forsook my usual desire for makeup and more Cd's, and silently petitioned Father Christmas to, instead, bring my daddy home.

One night, after sitting around the table for dinner, Mum asked me to run outside to check the mail. I rewrapped my chitenge tightly around my waist, slipped on my shoes and did as I was told. I skipped my way to the little mail box at the end of the street. When I reached in to retrieve our letters, my hands slid across the silky surface of whatever was at the top of the stack. When I pulled it out, I stood there frozen, my eyes glued to the photograph staring back at me. I saw him there, my daddy, his naked body reflecting back at me. I saw the things his now oversized clothing covered up on our visits to the prison; those small holes in his arms, those lines across his chest, like long uneven brushstrokes. My ears were ringing with the phantom sounds an object makes when it connects with flesh.

"What did they do to you?" I whispered to that figure standing there in the picture with his hands covering his genitals.

I ran back to the house and entered the living room with my chest heaving. Before Mum could chastise me in annoyance, I shoved the picture into her hands. She looked it over in silence before sending me to my room. I did not know whether I should tell my sisters what I had seen or not. I did not want to frighten them. I tried to keep it to myself but the pain was clamoring inside like a set of percussions, and I eventually whispered my secret to big sister. I looked at her after I had said it, waiting for her to offer some kind of reassurance or explanation. But what could she say? No one prepares you for what you will say after you realize that your father is being tortured regularly. Later on in life, I would read articles about what he had endured inside the walls of that prison, about how it had ignited an anti-torture passion inside of him. I would read about the rods and cables and wires, and those words would make sense of the marks I had seen in that picture. I did not sleep that night.

When we returned to school after the break, South Africa no longer felt the same. The gates of the school were not able to keep out the anxiety. I still played and laughed and batted my eyelashes at the Rugby players, but I also chewed my fingernails absentmindedly and would erupt into tearful fits on occasion. One of my teachers took notice of the change in me, pulled me aside and asked me to tell her what was happening. I wanted to; she had the kindest eyes and the most comforting spirit, but the words were lodged in my throat. I was not good at talking about the things that were happening inside me. No one had ever asked me and I wasn't sure if I could trust anyone. I knew the words but it was like my mouth did not know how to form them into sounds. She did not push me, but told me that if I wanted to tell her, she would listen. Eventually after weeks of weighing the options, I wrote her a letter. I did not tell her everything, or even the worst parts. That first letter was a test. She did not ask me about it, taking the cue that it was difficult to speak these things into open air. Instead she wrote me a letter back. I can still remember the pale blue color of her stationary, my first experience of having the pain validated. I wrote and wrote and wrote, all of my darkness manifested on wide ruled sheets of notebook paper. It temporarily lightened my load and restored South Africa to it's former status as a beacon of safety and freedom.

When half term descended, we boarded a plane yet again and spent the next two weeks carting food from the apartment to the prison. We took a boxed birthday cake, trimmed in white icing and royal blue roses and sat across from him as we sang happy birthday. I was relieved to find that daddy had regained some weight and that the pillowiness of his frame seemed to be returning. His eyes were no longer tinged with that somewhere in between yellow and brown that indicated poor health. Most of all, it was clear his passion had returned. They could not beat that out of him as they had hoped. I have learned I am the same as him in that way. I looked at him and could see the wheels of reformation twisting inside his brain. I was one quarter proud, one quarter frustrated and the rest of me was numb. Passion was synonymous with absence and I wondered, if he ever got to come home, would we lose him again to his cause. The answer seemed obvious.

At the apartment us girls quarantined ourselves into our shared bedroom. Mum had a new friend and his presence made my spine tingle. He walked into the house with groceries in his arms and a wide smile across his face. Mum would smile back. I could feel her flirtatious energy leaving her body and landing against his in a way that enticed him into some kind of stupor. It was uncomfortable to watch. When he turned toward us girls, his arms extended outward in an invitation, we shuffled our feet closer to him and reluctantly pressed ourselves into his embrace. His arms felt like snakes pressing the life out of my body. Mum hurried off into the kitchen and put all her skills to good use to prepare a meal for supper. We sat at the table, the two of them sitting close together. I wanted to excuse myself into the bedroom. The way he touched her at the dinner table made me want to squeeze my eyes shut. I did not know what to do, or think for that matter. I watched as his hands snuck into hidden places and wondered with my eyes open, trying to untangle the intertwining lines of love and lust and duty. I didn't know if there was a difference anymore. They all seemed to manifest into the same sounds and forms in front of my eyes.

AFTER YOU WALKED OUT

After you walked out
    Wearied from years of his closed fists against your cheekbones
    The instability of his changeable affection
    and the sorrow you suffered in silence, at the knowledge of his
other women
    How he, perhaps, touched them with the tenderness
    He had once pledged - unshakably - to you
    Before whatever moment paralyzed the love between you
    Then the man came -
    With arms tipped unnaturally
    Weighed down with the perishables he'd purchased
    In exchange for permission
    To put his hands into the holes of your oversized dress
    Reaching underneath and inside and making you moan and purr
    With eyes anchored on your little girl
    Instructed to sit across the dining room table
    Silently
    After you walked out
    When the man was finished, his crooked fingers glistened
    Slick with the remnants of you
    You laughed with tears frozen
    Like cement, at the tips of your crows feet
    While he wiped himself carelessly
    On the napkin you'd folded so delicately
    Tossing it coarsely on the plate
    Nodding toward you to clear his place
    After you walked out
    He made love to you in the shadowy blackness
    While we sat huddled in the room beside yours
    Their sobs shook their bodies
    I was tempted to weep in despair
    But by the time the man came—

I'd already learned that these were merely the duties
Of a woman in love
Or a woman in need.

This was the routine for one whole year: back and forth between school and home, the prison and home, back to school etc. I was not joking when I told you that children are adaptable, because after a while the shock of daddy's imprisonment wore off and disintegrated into another part of life. When we reached the end of third term, we packed up our bags and returned home for another winter break. There was commotion when we arrived, mouths flapping with news that daddy's release was imminent. Their commotion did not stir my insides. I had given up dealing in potential outcomes. I would feel what I felt when and if I needed to feel it. When all their commotion finally culminated in a court date, Mum picked out our best dresses once again. We piled into the back of the car, our trusty driver manning the wheel as usual and made our way to the courthouse. We sat outside the courtroom while Mum went inside. We could not hear what was being said, but when that gavel landed, we heard that hidden room erupt into sounds that meant freedom. When daddy emerged from the courtroom we sprinted to him. We were there in the newspaper beside him the following day, restored to our position of paper power.

After that the man disappeared as quickly as he came, and Mum positioned herself beside daddy once again, as the wife of a falsely accused politician was expected to do. We packed our things and moved back into the house at the farm. Once, the front of that house was adorned with lush greenery and flowers that split the driveway in two. Big sister and I would race around the opposing halves, pumping our arms hard and fast, determined to make it to the front door first. But on this drive back home, the land's vibrancy seemed to have withered away just like the fat underneath Daddy's skin, like the land itself was starving for something. As we all were.

Daddy's friends and colleagues piled into the house day after day, shaking his hand and patting his back and congratulating him on surviving such an ordeal. Everyone seemed to be talking as if the scars on his body were something to be capitalized on. I wanted to shove them out of our house and bolt the door closed.

We spent that Christmas and New Years with extended family, all the adults pouring beer and champagne down their throats, toasting the good fortune of Daddy's release, the miracle of a brand new year. I sat in his lap as usual and snuck my privileged sips of pink champagne. I pressed my nose into his white shirt, savoring the way he smelled clean and familiar, that old prison musk having left him. That night he whispered into my ear,

"Everything I do, I do for you girls. For your future, and to make you proud."

I hugged him tightly, wrapping both arms around his neck. In that moment it felt as if I was cradling him in my arms and not the other way around. I wanted to whisper to him that he did not have to work so hard to make me proud. I wanted to tell him that the only thing he had to do now to make me proud was stay.

I wonder now if I should have.

As anticipated, he went back to work almost immediately, probably against the doctor's orders. The guest house on the farm turned into a political gathering place. As I walked by, on my way to the swimming pool, I saw the hunched backs of men dressed like Daddy, their heads crammed together as they pondered how to turn their ideas into something tangible, like new laws and regulations. Occasionally I would poke my head in, maybe just to make sure he was still there and still a free man. He would pat my head and I would run off so that I did not throw his work rhythm off kilter. Just like that, life straightened itself back into some variation of normal. Us girls spent the last days of winter break running around outside and shaking our heads at the peach trees that had given up bearing fruit. To be clear, winter is a term to be understood loosely in this context. It was swimming weather all year round back then. We snuck into the chicken coops and picked up the tiny chicks and cradled their warmth in our hands. We pretended to have wings like those little birds and flapped our arms around, chasing each other until we collapsed in a pile of soaring laughter. That was the winter of horseback rides up and down our dirt driveway, and of watching grown up films on mute on the television so we would not get caught. It was the winter I slipped on water in our kitchen and was knocked unconscious. I still have the bump on the back of my head. Big sister told me that Mum had tried to slap me awake after it happened, but that my eyes did not flutter open from the impact of her hand on my cheek, so it is one slap I do not, gratefully, remember. Though we did not know it at the time, these were the last of our days at the house on the hill and I am grateful that we spent them so well. When the break finally came to an end, big sister and I patted baby sister on the head, reminding her to keep watch of the chicks, boarded the plane as usual and glided from one world back into another.

ONE DAY, lost as I normally was in the safety of South Africa, as I let my best friend put my braided hair in high pig tails like Baby Spice, our dorm mom rushed into the room in a huff. I ignored her because it was very much her nature to enter rooms breathing hard, often unnecessarily. I imagined she would walk through the room on her way to find whoever the culprit was, but this time she stopped in front of me, her face flushed some unnamed shade in between purple and red.

"Your father is on the phone," she said quietly.

I didn't know what to make of this. His voice was never the one on the other side of the line, perhaps I had even forgotten it was possible for a father to wonder about you while you were away for months at a time. In the three years we spent at that school he had only visited once. He picked us up and took us to the mall, fully outfitted in a suit. I shook my head in embarrassment. It was unquestionably uncool for fathers to dress so formally while walking through Woolworths or sitting through Titanic with their daughters. He carted us around the mall, filling our pockets with sweets and our stomachs with chips, and of course, he filled our ears with stories of future reunions. When he left I did not cry as I anticipated I would. I squeezed him tightly and watched him drive away, turned and sprinted back to the dorms to show off my treasures. At school his absence did not bother me. I enjoyed the vast separateness of my home life and my boarding school life. So when all of a sudden his voice was there on the other side of the line, my mind rocketed off in a million directions. I took in dorm mom's face, scanning and trying to get a better message from her, but she gave nothing away. I tiptoed past her into her tiny apartment and pressed the phone against my ear.

My dad was never the kind of man to beat around the bush, to kill time with platitudes. He got straight to the point. It typically earned my respect, but in this moment he could have, perhaps, softened the blow with a small joke, or maybe a simple hello.

"Your mother has been shot," he said directly.

Now my insides quivered violently, my emotions oscillated between grief, terror and God help me, a small sliver of relief (I know, I am not proud of it, but I promised I would tell you the truth). I was not accustomed to making judgements about my own feelings, so I remained silent, waiting for him to tell me the rest. He said nothing, our breaths instead passed into each other's ears in slow motion.

"Is she dead?" I asked finally, no longer able to bear the stillness.

SHE WASN'T DEAD.
    She was badly injured —
    but she wasn't dead.

I GOT the information I needed in order to make sense of what was happening and got off the phone with him. I put the phone on the receiver gently and ran barefoot across the campus. I ran with one hand pressed against my chest tightly, as if holding all the pieces of the story firmly so none of them would tumble out through my fingertips. I kept going - past the cafeteria, through the grass where we had played made up games on the weekends, under the arched courtyard entrance where I imagined kissing one of the rugby boys and straight into the chapel. I knew I would find my sister there, she and the older girls telling secrets in the pews. I barged in, my chest heaving painfully. I slowed as I approached where big sister was sitting. I registered the faint look of annoyance on her face. She did not like for me to insert myself into her antics with the older girls.

"Mummy's been shot," I spat out before she could chastise me for interrupting. I used the same vacant tone daddy had used on the phone and tried to remain calm.

She screamed, collapsing into a fit of tears. I told her the story. I cried while I described my baby sister waiting quietly, hidden away in the bathtub where she had been playing when the men used their fists against our front door and began questioning my mum about the whereabouts of my father.

She didn't know, she'd told them. And she wasn't lying. No one ever knew where my father was until he came home. She had offered them money and her jewelry, perhaps one of her sparkling rings I tried on in secret, but those items were inconsequential. They had come for the politicians blood. These were the consequences of his involvement in politics: imprisonment and threats of death. I felt the rage climbing up my throat as I told the story, despising my dad's commitment to something that put us so consistently in danger in more ways than one. I wanted him to let someone else fight for his cause. I wanted him to come home. I shook my head to clear the haze of silent rage and continued:

THEY WERE JUST LEAVING when mum stepped outside to make sure they were gone.

AND THEN THE shock of little pellets entering her body, the impact causing her frame to fall forward onto the marble veranda, her dark blood spilling out like a carpet underneath her. I imagined her shallow breath as she laid there, utterly human, utterly alone. I felt tears drip down my cheeks and onto my chest as the words spilled out of my mouth. My arms itched to reach into my own story and hold her, tell her it was going to be okay.

Somehow she managed to pick her punctured body up off the

ground and drag herself back up the steps, through the house and to the bathroom where she had told her baby to wait quietly. I can hardly let myself imagine what my five year old sister looked up and saw.

I don't know how, but she put them both into the car and drove the windy couple of miles to the home of our nearest neighbor. I don't know how she managed to stay alive. When she told the story in latter years, she would say she found herself passing out at the wheel, the pain stealing the last of her resolve to stay awake. But somehow she kept coming back to life. There is not a moment in existence that better captures my mother's resilience than this.

"She is badly injured," I whispered in conclusion. "But she isn't dead."

Pause.

"We have to go home."

WE BOARDED a plane soon after and returned home. Daddy did not meet us at the airport, but our driver was like family, having been privy to secrets whispered between my big sister and me in the back seat confines of that blue Benz. He drove us down familiar roads until we stopped in front of the square hospital. The inside smelled like a cologne with notes of death and undertones of chemical grade sanitizer. We stepped into the small room to find her reduced to a pile of bandages, the dried blood from the places the metal had sailed through her skin like an abstract painting dancing around her body. She didn't immediately stir. I moved timidly to stand beside her hospital bed, disturbed by how human she seemed, lying there with the beeping machines standing guard. I wanted to reach out and stroke her still forehead but my hands would not move. I wanted to crawl in the bed beside her, inhabit the circle of her arms for one moment. I felt my affection for her pumping inside me, my thoughts spinning into a prayer, a plea, that she would awaken a softer version of herself; that this sleep could be a second birth. A second chance, maybe.

When she opened her eyes, a sheet of rage hung around her

eyelids, concealing the hurt, pain and fear I imagined were threatening to break her. This time I did not blame her. I knew what it was like to allow rage to focus you, the determination that sort of anger held hands with. I did not blame her because I saw that her back was shoved into a corner, that she could either let the agony come and overtake her, or she could survive. Mum was even more skilled at surviving than I was. When daddy was in the room, I watched her examine him in silence, the air thick and strained. I watched them and my senses informed me that something had died on the veranda that day when the men came with their guns strung over their shoulders. Things would never be the same. They could not be. I watched my daddy in silence, this time my anger outweighed my love for him. He offered me his usual toothy grin, but I looked away, overcome with some feeling I could not yet put words to. It was as if, for the first time ever, reality twisted itself into something foreign. As if for those strained minutes in the hospital, daddy transformed into the villain and Mum into some version of a woman I could relate to. Weren't we both bleeding as a result of him, or rather, as a result of the absence of him? I still can't be sure.

WHERE ARE YOU GOING

where are you going, papa

didn't I wave the tattered flag of your cause?
    didn't I champion you?
    didn't I send you off with your briefcase
    and a cursive note hidden in your breast pocket?
    didn't I kiss you on the cheek?
    didn't I watch your tires resurrect the sleeping dirt?
    didn't you honk twice as you drove away,
    all in the name of a better tomorrow?

You told me your arms were a border—
    A safe country in which I could build my home
    You said inside that country I was the queen
    You placed a golden crown on my head and dignified me:
    The very triumph of your life

where are you going, papa

didn't I forgive the way your hands branded her neck?
    didn't I hate her to make more room inside to love you?
    didn't I violate my own good sense
    in order to remain faithful to you,
    a man who only remained faithful to himself
    in the end?

You told me your love was a broad place—
    A field in which I could lie down and rest without intermission
    You said one day I would have more than the carcass of your affection
    Inside your arm country, I would no longer be a refugee
    And no harm would befall your baby

where are are you going, papa

didn't I pledge allegiance to your flag?
    didn't I wear your name with pride?
    didn't I choose you in spite of your wandering eye,
    or the way you walked home with the smell of other children
    lingering in your clothes?

Where have you been, papa

didn't I decline to see you as the genesis of this?
    refuse to blame you for the way her hands made marks on my skin
    how when you were finished with her, she used the iron you
left hot
    to turn around and sear my flesh
    didn't I?
    …
    where have you gone, papa?

In the backseat of the car, daddy already having sped off to this meeting or that appearance, or to wherever he went during the day, I noticed that we were not winding roads that lead to the outstretched land called home. Instead, we pulled into a gated cluster of small homes. I glanced at the driver in confusion. He looked back but offered no explanation. Out of the front door came Great Aunt, baby sister walking timidly beside her. We embraced each other and I imagine I must have cried but I cannot be sure. I wish I had knelt down on the pavement and looked baby sister in the face and asked her to recite back to me what she had witnessed. How she had kept herself from crying out as she sat in the stale bathtub water. I should have validated her pain. I should have asked her what a gun sounds like when it fires, if she had felt the impact through the walls of the house. I should have held her and let her soak my shoulder with tears. I wish I'd known then all the skills that are so much a part of me now. I wish I'd known. But back then I did not know, so I did not ask. It is one of my greatest regrets. I grabbed her tiny hand in mine and we walked numbly into another new home.

It was smaller than I was accustomed to, but still, beautiful in its simplicity. The walls were crisp and white, the perfect canvas for a family to outfit with their own unique touches. A painting here, Persian rug slid underneath one corner of a coffee table, gold leaf mirror above the vanity. My favorite feature was the staircase that wound up to the second floor, light streaming in from the huge windows at the top of the landing. It might have been the sort of home I would dream of settling into in the future, making a little pile of pillows underneath the window where I could read my books and write my stories. Our bedrooms were upstairs, some of our toys stuffed inside. It was unclear to me how the transition had happened so quickly, but as I have said, paper power has its usefulness.

The living room on the first floor was full of pillows and heavy blankets. The lights were kept dim and the drapes stayed drawn. We were told that when mum returned home she would not be able to carry herself up the stairs for some time, and would be using the space as her own private room. Great Aunt shook her finger sternly in our

75

faces, reminding us that we should not pester her, remain quiet and out of the way. I simply nodded, swallowing down the urge to tell her that staying out of the way was not a novel way of being.

Daddy came later, a nurse behind him, helping Mum into the house and onto the couch. She would not look at him, though he asked if she was comfortable. He draped his arms around my shoulders and pulled me into an embrace. For once I did not feel myself relax into him. When he left us that night, returning to his work or to his cause, I shut a part of myself off from him. When he made his promises I only let them enter seventy five percent of me, but the other twenty five percent was off limits. That part was angry and bitter and suddenly despised the number of times I'd watched him walk away, leaving me to listen intently for the scrape of his keys against the deadbolt. I did not understand how he could leave us while knowing that Mum's life had just been threatened. Did he not have the urge to stay, guard the door throughout the night and make sure no harm came to his babies? Apparently not. Besides, he had men who could do the job for him. I hated how easily he seemed to hand off the responsibility of fathering us to waiting hands.

The next weeks passed mostly in silence. We were not made to go back to school while Mum healed and besides, there were the whispers beginning of moves out of the country in order to maintain our safety. Mum laid on the couch, wincing and moaning every time she moved. The sounds twisted up the winding staircase and landed in our room interrupting our games. I wanted to help her but I knew better. The living room carried a putrid smell, a thick moldy stench that was probably the result of the towels on the ground on which mum continued to spit the bile that insisted on sliding its way up her throat. It made be shudder every time she did it.

We spent the days playing quietly, or sneaking into the living room to ask if we could take a walk or play outside. Once a week daddy would send the driver to pick us up, squeezing us into his schedule for lunch. We sat in restaurants eating fried chicken or samosas while he asked us how we were doing. I answered dully, keeping my eyes down to conceal my tears. I looked at his hands in contempt as he procured this gift or that from those hidden pocket depths of his; an eyeshadow palette this week, a pack of our favorite chewing gum the next. It was difficult not to shout at him; the void inside kept expanding into something that made it difficult to maintain my well mannered nature. He, however, continued to operate as if nothing had changed. He made his promises and he left, back to more important matters.

It was not long after that that our ears began being filled with whispers of the word "America." It happened as Mum regained her strength, wincing as she aligned her torso over her knees and began shuffling around the small home. She gathered her spit soaked towels and she gathered her pride and moved herself upstairs to her previously unoccupied room. She and Great Aunt sat in the living room speaking softly in tongues that us girls never learned, but 'America' rang out clearly, unwilling to be disguised by native sounds. Big sister and I had our secret meetings too. We wondered why we were not being sent back to boarding school. We wondered about the passport pictures and the paperwork and those words like "refugee" and "political asylee." For this part of the story it was as if we were spectators standing on the edge of a platform and merely observing as the train of our lives was rushing ahead to some unknown destination. I was there, of course, but I cannot tell you exactly how months of planning and applying and waiting and watching culminated into our feet in the middle of the airport tarmac, boarding passes in hand, carryon luggage on our backs, my little monkey keychain dangling off the side. I cannot tell you because no one was telling me, you understand? All I know is once there was a house with crisp white walls and then there was the feeling of the airplane seat underneath my bottom and my ears popping as the wheels left the ground and hid themselves inside the belly of the plane—

AND THEN THERE WAS AMERICA.

The plane was crowded, all of us sitting with our sweaty elbows rubbing awkwardly against each other. Baby sister was vomiting up the cold mashed potatoes they had placed on the tray tables in front of us and Mum was screaming at her to stop, blaming our supposedly voracious appetites for her illness. I sat frozen and upright with my back rigid against the airplane seat. I could still smell my daddy's cologne on my t-shirt. I wanted to open a window and call out to him, strap on a parachute and fall until I landed back inside his arms.

My eyes became crowded with tears.

I cocked my head against the half open window and peered into the blackness. I kept thinking about pretending to be a mermaid in our swimming pool while daddy chased us. He'd shake his head as water bounced off the surface of his moisture shrunken afro. I kept thinking about South Africa, about the boy I should have let myself press my lips against whether he wanted me to or not. About our marble veranda, once this beacon in my mind where daddy had taught me to fly, now stained crimson with mum's blood, a grave reminder of all the reasons we could not stay.

These were the first thoughts as the plane glided out of Africa and into America. This great land that people had whispered about for months, a glossy representation of safety, of prosperity, of potential. And yet, as the wheels scraped against the tar and as the plane skidded clumsily to a stop, I felt certain that we had left any hope of safety standing in the tarmac thousands of miles away. There had been tears as I forced myself to let go of him. There had also been promises, my dad's tongue like the quill of a fountain pen, constantly adding more declarations to a constitution that would never come to pass.

"We will see each other soon," he spoke into our ears, "I will join you there and then we will all come home."

That is the way he is frozen inside my mind. His white collared shirt tucked neatly into his black trousers, his curly hair cropped tight against his scalp, and his mouth frozen in mid formation of the last lie he ever told me. I accepted his hope and put it into my pocket like a treasure. I looked at his smile, full of reassurance, and put it into my pocket too. In hindsight I should have folded him like a t-shirt and tucked him into my carry on luggage. But then, no one had informed me of the finality of this rushed interaction. When it is the last time you will see someone of such significance, someone ought to tell you, don't you agree?

Much later, when I was eighteen, Great Aunt told me she had been sitting beside him when the last of his life exited his body through clenched teeth. She said he had remained stubborn until the end, clutching onto those final moments until his fingertips turned white. She told me that the sickness had eaten away at him, slowly, leaving his once plush teddy bear frame on the edge of decay.

She said, a hint of tentativeness creeping into her voice, that he had kept calling Mum for years. He had kept asking to speak to his girls.

"They do not want to speak to you," she'd offered, her voice cold and unmoving.

The shock felt like a blade through the gut. Sharp. Cold. Precise. My heart still stops now as if I am hearing it again for the first time. I did not think it was possible for her to hurt me in this way anymore. It is likely my fault for continuing to underestimate her.

My chest was constricted, as if suddenly I was attempting to suck air through a clogged straw. I was exhausted, the weight of one more thing feeling like it could pull me under and away. I would have let it. Do you know that feeling you get when life has just run you over one too many times, and all you want to do is lay down somewhere warm and whisper into whatever blackness keeps coming, "okay, fine, you win. I give up?" That is what you would see here.

I wanted to scream into the receiver. I wanted her to untell me.

"UNTELL ME," I wanted to shout, over and over until the truth unclasped itself from my insides.

I swallowed down the ache. I did my best to get off the phone quickly and diplomatically. I let my body descend against the kitchen cabinets until I was on the floor. I stayed there. With the cool tile pressing on my calves. With the day growing black outside. I stayed there. I tried to keep my mind from playing his final moments like a movie behind my closed eyes but it would not listen.

So I stayed, weighed down with my own bitter grief and watched.

I watched that once broad smiling presidential candidate lying still on yellowing hospital covers. I saw the way the quivers continued to pass through his body in spite of the blankets piled on top of his now shrunken frame. I watched how the hospital gown hung limply and away from the bones in his clavicle like a hula hoop. I smelled that faint vinegar smell hanging around the room. His once smooth brow was creased, perhaps lined by the impending reality of death.

He was in pain and I wanted this mind movie to end.

He spoke quietly, a mildly disoriented narrative of all the things that he had accomplished, all the things he had experienced. He was proud of the life he had lived. He was proud of the fight he had fought. He would, perhaps, do it all again.

There is just one thing:

"I will never understand why my children did not want to talk to me," he whispered, the pitch of his voice rising slightly, as if he was asking a question, to whom, I cannot be sure.

The pain was so heavy the tears could not seem to squeeze out around it.

I felt it too as my mind imagined his final moments. Me and my daddy on split screens: one side - him collecting ragged breaths into his body, wilting away while believing I wanted nothing to do with him. On the other - me listening and listening for those wingtip shoes against the pavement, those metal keys against the deadbolt.

Tell me, do you think he knows the truth now? Do you think he knows that I had been waiting for him all along?

The scream I released obliterated the silence of the kitchen.

Let me be honest: I am, at this moment, tempted to leave out from the story, the rage that overtook my entire body. After all these years it had sprouted into something thick and black. I have a violent streak no one would ever associate with me. I am too accommodating, too sweet, and I would like you to continue to think of me in that way. I don't want to ruin it by telling you about how I felt myself fill entirely with heat, how I longed to throw my fists against my mother's door, and, when she opened, throw my fists against her body until she bled. I am tempted not to describe the way my hands trembled at the thought of punishing her for every thing she had stolen from me, all the ways my choice and volition had been violated. How I wanted to tear her into shreds, one piece for every thing she had taken that I would never get back. I can never get them back, do you understand me?

I don't want you to know how hatred eclipsed any good in me and all that was left was a desperate desire for vengeance.

I don't want you to know because she is supposed to be the monster and not me.

PLEASE GIVE ME A MINUTE.

UNDONE

I'm coming undone.
My meticulously placed sutures are rupturing.
I'm afraid to expose what I've taken years learning to shut away.
I smell of you beneath this well formed armor.
You're still breathing in there.
Parasite
You're eating me dry
And I want to kill you with my uncaged-
Rage
I want to reach in there and choke you the way you have choked me
I want to rip you apart
I want to hear you whimper
Whisper
Beg me
Like I begged you to--
Stop
My ears are roaring
Alive with malice
Contempt
All the lessons of submission
Obedience
Fall away
I'm justifying myself with this hatred
Till I'm spent
And you have gorged yourself on my sin
I've mangled myself with my bitterness and deceit
Bloodied by my blindness
Whimpering
Whispering
I know I will never kill you this way
But the rage is electrifying
Momentarily.

I found out about his death two and a half years earlier, two months before my sixteenth birthday. Outside it was finally turning into spring, although that night the air was brisk, still clutching onto the last shreds of winter. It was the weekend before the garage sale. I'd spent the afternoon reluctantly flipping through my things, trying to decide which items to part with. Foster sister, six at the time, kept crying on the kitchen floor, outraged that she would be forced to watch another child walk away with one of her Barbies. It was getting late and foster mom was standing by the stove throwing dinner together, probably spaghetti, which I hated, having eaten it at least twice a week for too long.

Then her phone ringing.

She listened as the person on the other side spoke and then excused herself silently into the cold garage. I sat there waiting, somehow my senses on high alert. I was by now used to the way the air sounds when your life is about to experience another sharp twist. It hums a song you have been trying to forget. I think I gripped the counter as a way to stabilize myself. I can't be sure.

Now the door twisting open.

Life changes always announced themselves with the twist of a door knob, it seemed. Her southern sweetness had been replaced by a look of foreboding. She had something to say but she didn't want to tell me. I helped her by asking shakily.

There is not yet in existence an easy way to relay this sort of information to a person. You don't get a course that prepares you just in case you have to let someone know that their daddy is no longer living. To tell a girl that he is not going to be coming. To let someone know that there is no longer a need to watch the airplanes flying across the sky with your fingers crossed and your breath held, because he is not coming. He is not ever coming.

They say that before death your entire life flashes before your eyes, clear like a vision. But what about the things you see when your daddy's life is snuffed out so suddenly? What about how your mind flashes to your wedding day, you in that ivory dress you have been dreaming about, and as you walk down to meet whoever is waiting on the other side, you reach to loop your gloved arm into the crook of your daddy's elbow,

BUT HE IS NOT THERE.

I HEARD hope's door slam with a bang.

I memorialized him that night while kneeling on the concrete in the freezing garage, slapping neon price stickers on knick knacks to be sold. My mouth was in autopilot, telling story after story but without feeling anything. I let myself laugh as I recalled his silliness, and the way he would let me sneak out of bed and spin me around while I was enclosed safely in his arms. For a while I talked fast enough to outrun the pain. But pain is a skilled bounty hunter, and trust me, you cannot run forever.

It was the image of his stillness that finally tipped the tears over my eyelids. I had never witnessed the color a brown person turns when they are no longer breathing, so I had to use my imagination. Once the first fat tears fell, they would not stop. I had the urge to yell out to him that I was sorry. Maybe if we had not left, things would have turned out differently. I wanted to go to sleep and start every-thing again. I would not have left him that day in the airport. Or at the very least, I would not have let myself take that last goodbye for granted.

"I'm so sorry, daddy," every tear breathed, my whole body convulsing in agony. I wanted to crawl into the coffin beside him and press myself against his ribs, to join him in death's peaceful stillness. I did not want to feel anymore.

After that, there was only Luther Vandross' "Dance with my Father," floating out of the stereo on repeat, my sobs ebbing and flowing as the song eased in and out of the chorus. I typed daddy's name into the search engine with blurry vision. I read all the articles that were written, all the words used to describe him. I memorized them. I stewed in my shame, jealous that reporters seemed to know how to describe him better than I did. I felt cold as I read that he was survived by five daughters, the words confirming what I had, in secret overheard, and punctuating how little I knew about the man.

The pendulum swung violently between sorrow and anger, and I did not pause to feel any of the things in the middle. Grief is the strangest cocktail of emotion. I spent whole days so infuriated I could not register the agony underneath it. I hated him, I hated him for the choices he had made, that he had put us on that plane and had not regretted it until it was too late. I wanted to throw my body against his and educate him on the cost of his absence. To exhume his body, bring it back to life again and hurl objects at him until he wept at the impact.

I just wanted to hold him accountable for something. I didn't want to be the sorry one. I needed him to look me in the eyes and tell me he was sorry he ever let me go. I had been waiting for him for years. Waiting for him to extend those long brown arms out toward me in an invitation.

I would have run to him. After all this time, I still would have run to him.

FORGIVE ME. I don't mean to confuse you. It is just that this story has legs and sometimes it gets away from me.

Where was I? Oh yes, America.

I DON'T THINK I ever heard Mum speak about her sister. I'd done my puzzling together and had discerned that their relationship was tense. No one ever told stories with directness, but I was nosy and I was good at blending in, often pushing my barbies as close to the door as I could and pretending to be immersed in their micro world. But I was learning. I was always learning, soaking up information to add into my mind map at the end of the day.

Auntie had been living in America for years, initially moving there to attend college. She fell in love with an American man and decided not to return. It did not surprise my family. I'd heard words like impulsive being used to describe her.

I learned, through whispers sneaking inside cracked doors, that my daddy had also gone to college in America. I learned some other things about him; about his first love, the other children who shared half my blood. America, it seemed, was where people went to fall in love.

Then all of a sudden we were flying away from the only home I had ever known only to move in with that very sister, an aunt I had never known. This epitomized the unspoken rules about family, the unspoken expectations. Even if you hated the very person who shared your blood, even if they had wounded you beyond what one could imagine, when and if they needed you, you were expected to respond. Admittedly there is a sweetness to rules of this nature, a loyalty that entwined people together despite violations of safety. But as you can probably hear, there's also a darkness to being bonded in a way that minimizes safety and choice.

But I am getting ahead of myself again.

Auntie met us at the airport. She came alone, although I had been told that she had one child and a new husband, her second. She wrapped her arms around us, her broad smile attempting to soften the vertigo resulting from this abrupt tilting of reality. We hefted our luggage through the bustling airport, twisting and turning as we made our way outside. I held on to my big sister's shirt corner so that the crowds did not carry me off like those suitcases on the carousel.

The Atlanta air felt like an unwelcome hug, that damp, sticky heat reaching its overbearing arms out and holding on longer than necessary. I had never felt anything similar. The short walk to the car left me heaving and starving for more air. We drove on immaculately paved roads, huge highways bending into and around each other. I had never seen so many cars competing for space. When Auntie used her foot on the brakes, I clung to my sister's arms terrified that we were about to collide into the vehicle in front of us. She laughed and glanced back at me through the rear view mirror.

I did not know what to make of her. Imagining that she and mum

88

were products of the same womb, that twin blood coursed through their veins was one puzzle I have yet to piece together. She seemed unafraid of her sister, despite the unyielding scowl on mum's face. She joked and spilled stories one after another, and filled the stuffy car with something I could not identify. I felt nauseous. I wanted to warn her. I wanted to ask her to stop before she pushed mum too far. But she seemed unaware of the rules, or perhaps she didn't care about them.

As we turned into the neighborhood, I took in my new surroundings. I looked at the suburb homes, sitting side by side in such close proximity. We weaved through quiet streets, all the houses matching as if they had been stamped out of a mold in a factory. People have asked me about the differences between Africa and America, asked me if I had a car or running water. They've asked me if there were lions in my backyard, how I dealt with the feral dogs running through the streets. I have always replied with a chuckle and said simply, we had more land.

We parked the car in the vacant rectangle of the driveway. I stepped out onto the small square of grass that she called her "front yard," and felt the walls of America pushing in on me. I missed my guava trees. The front door swung open and my cousin ran out, her small body filled with double the energy of her mother. She spoke to us as if we had been longtime friends while Aunt was hushing her and reminding her that we were likely tired from our journey.

Their house was inviting, pictures and trophies on the shelves, the faint smell of vanilla occupying the air. My sisters and I piled into one of the spare bedrooms, a queen sized bed pushed up against the wall and a small twin mattress on the carpet. My mother took another room for herself, and I sighed in relief that one of us was not expected to share her space. We sat with our feet hanging off the bed, my sisters and I, looking at each other without speaking. I watched a shadow of resignation slide across their faces. I knew there would be no conversation to check in about how we were managing the adjustment, no arms to hold us through the homesickness. And so, six feet hanging off the bed, we nodded, swallowed back the sadness and walked head-first into our new life.

Later that night Uncle came home from work. He was tall and round, his belly often knocking into things as he turned quickly. My cousin ran into his arms before he set his briefcase on the ground. I looked out the window, trying to gulp back the knot forming inside my throat. I wanted to peer around his large frame and see my daddy walking in behind him. He greeted us with handshakes, asking about the plane ride and shaking his head with pity after hearing that baby sister had been unwell.

Standing in the living room, our family on one side, theirs on the other, I could hear the tension popping like firecrackers. I could sense the competing ways of life surveilling one another. In that house, when my cousin broke the rules, she got a spanking. She cried as she walked to her room and waited for her mom or dad to follow her, the spanking spoon resting lazily in their hands. She cried as the spoon tapped against her bottom. And then they hugged. I never saw her on her knees begging for re-entry into the folds of love, I never heard the crack as the spoon splintered in half. I had the feeling of wanting to walk over to the other side of the living room and make my home across the invisible line.

WE MOVED to Atlanta in the first stretches of summertime. Children filled the culdesac, riding circles around each other on their bikes and sprinting through sprinklers to keep cool. School had always been a year round occurrence for me, breaks scattered throughout the year. In America school closed for the entire summer. I was unenthused by this change, ten whole weeks at home sounding like a bad dream. Auntie made us take walks in the early afternoon, up and down the winding roads of the neighborhood. She said it would help us adjust to the air, patting our shoulders when we complained of fatigue. Having her around felt like a buffer. Mum retreated, often hiding herself in her bedroom with glasses of gin and tonic, maybe trying to nurse her own shock and grief into submission. It is bizarre, but not impossible, to imagine that mum was sitting on her new bed, her feet dangling off the edge, tears falling into her lap. Maybe her body still ached from the pellets they could not remove, maybe her heart was sore from leaving home, maybe she missed my daddy too. This is one of those moments that would be better observed on split screens. Here you might find that mum and I were mirror images, both grief stricken and afraid, both surviving in the only ways we knew how. But we will never know.

Two weeks into our stay Mum told us she would be returning to Africa in a week's time. She said she needed to finalize some affairs. She and daddy were selling our house. It felt illegal, that home belonging to anyone besides us.

"But daddy said we would all go back home," I said.

Her mouth disappeared into a thin line as she glared at me. I knew that was the end of the discussion.

Daddy had lied while looking directly into my eyes it seemed.

She left a week later, as promised, set to return at the end of summer. She closed the door behind her and the house stretched in liberation. With her gone I learned to laugh like my cousin. I sank into Auntie's embrace when she hugged me. She wanted to know about my dreams, about what I aspired to be when I was bigger, and I let myself tell her. On the weekends Uncle would push himself into the front door, groceries weighing his arms down. All six of us would crowd into their kitchen and make gumbo. Uncle used his big voice to shout orders to each of us. We'd go to work chopping vegetables and sausage and cleaning the heads of crawfish, Michael Jackson blaring from the stereo.

That was the first summer I learned about my sensitivity. I was desperate for affection, starving for it. But it also terrified me. The smallest things caused me to retreat and freeze out anyone who tried to come close. Auntie would ask me what was happening, asking me about my grudges, as she called them, but I couldn't explain it to her. I did not understand it myself. Thankfully she was patient and forgiving, letting me go away into my rage cocoon, accepting my apology when I emerged.

On Saturday nights we would pile into the car and drive to the newspaper factory, the musky scent of paper wrapping around us. Uncle worked weekdays in an office but on the weekends he delivered newspapers to make extra money. We spent our Saturday nights rolling the fat stack of inserts that made up the Sunday paper as our fingertips turned black from the ink. We bagged one after the other until we had enough to fill the trunk of his car, then rushed home to steal a few hours of sleep. He'd told big sister and I we could make the rounds with him and earn some spending money. He woke us up while it was still dark outside. We maneuvered around baby sister, threw on our running shoes and crawled into his car. He did the apartments first, dropping us off with a handful of newspapers and telling us which doors to drop them off at. I'd sprint up the stairs of the tall buildings and throw the papers down with precision, run back down, crawl into the car and do it all over again. Over and over until all the apartments had their papers. Then big sister and I would collapse in the back seat of the car, lay our heads against each other as he threw papers out of his open window to each of the houses on his round. I slept peacefully, that steady thump thump thump, paper landing on asphalt, a strange but comforting lullaby. He woke us when we arrived at the house, shoved our allowance into our palms and ushered us back to bed. We slept, our limbs weary from exertion, but only for a few hours, because every Sunday, without exception, we dressed and drove to service at the church where they were members.

They attended a charismatic black church, the music filling up the whole building like a pulse. The older ladies, in their wide hats, stood on shaky legs and raised their arms to the sky in worship. The preacher moved across the pulpit like it was a stage while the sermon stretched on and on until his feet had moved across every inch of the pulpit. My big sister and I joined the church step team. We practiced every Saturday, our feet tapping to the beat of Kirk Franklin. I was substandard, at best. My feet would not learn the steps fast enough, would not stomp hard enough, and so for those anticipated Sunday performances, I found myself relegated to the back. I envied the way my big sister already seemed to be finding her place in this new world. I felt betrayed as she left me to stand near new friends, and terrified that I was losing my best friend. I never told her.

I'd been attending church my whole life. Every Sunday I'd dressed in colorful dresses, my white frilly socks sticking out of well polished shoes, and driven to the small church in the capital city. I'd shaken hands with the president at the end of service, sang hymns beside leaders of the army. I clapped my hands at the right times, closed my eyes during prayers and turned to the correct pages in my small Bible. In South Africa, the boarding school had been Anglican. We were required to attend services every week. We'd giggle through them, laughing heartlessly at the headmaster's wife whose body shook from some unnamed illness. Those services were less colorful than the ones at home. Every week we'd say the same dry words, watching the friar walk back and forth in his white robe. What I'm saying is I'd heard about God my whole life, heard mum and daddy at times debating heatedly about their theological positions. But that first summer in Atlanta, I pleaded with him as if he was real and right in front of me. I sat in my pressed dress in front of the altar, I sobbed, I moved my lips in passionate supplication. I wanted him to make a way for me to stay with Auntie and Uncle even after mum returned to America. I didn't want to leave. I wanted to keep delivering newspapers. I wanted to keep making gumbo in the crowded kitchen. I wanted to keep going on little dates to the movies with Uncle, me leaning myself against him and shoving popcorn into my mouth. I could feel the summer gliding forward, kids already moaning about how many days were left until school started. I could feel my insides moaning too, mum's eventual return creeping closer and closer. Let me be clear here: it was not a shortage of love for Mum that was making my lips move in desperation. I loved her desperately. If I could have chosen softness from anyone, it would have been from her. It's just at the time, that option did not seem viable.

WHEN SHE DID RETURN it was evident that her remaining softness had deteriorated while she had been away. Her tolerance for Auntie had disappeared and they went to war with each other over their different approaches to everything, from food to discipline. Mum. noticing my affection for Uncle, spat allegations at me, accusing me of being inappropriately involved with him. Words like slut and whore do not leave your system with ease. They cling on like leeches underneath your skin. I reared back as she said them, full of self loathing. I felt dirty and sinful, convinced that I had crossed lines that I was not even aware existed. Was I a perpetrator? I was trying to make sense of where I had overstepped but could not seem to find the place. I kept grasping for safety but I always managed to get it wrong. It marked me. A decade later, I am still watchful, constantly evaluating myself with men, even those men who are safe. The remaining scraps of trust in myself fractured as the last insults left her lips.

We stayed longer than I imagined we would. We did not make gumbo on the weekends anymore. We were at times banned from those weekend newspaper runs as well. The summer, once sprinting toward an end now dragged by lazily. We spent the last days playing rock paper scissors trying to determine which of us would bravely knock on Mum's door and ask her if we could go swimming the next day. We'd of course learned when the best time to ask was. You had to wait until she had retired for the evening, catch her right between tipsy and drunk. Any sooner and it was a firm no, any later and she was unpredictable and completely unrestrained. But mum in that sweet spot was the most agreeable version of herself.

In America the end of summer is not marked by a reprieve from the heat. It is not marked by a slight chill in the air. No, in America the end of summer is marked by department stores stocking their shelves to the brim with pencils and pens and every color backpack you can imagine. We walked through the aisles with crinkled school supply lists clutched in our fingers. I'll tell you one thing, in Africa, school supplies were not so glamorous, and you did not have so many choices. A pencil was just a pencil, a practical means to an end. But in America, I learned, your choice of pen or backpack could earn you praise or rejection. Shopping for the start of school is an event. I felt anxious as I imagined what my first day would be like. I asked Auntie what to expect, I asked her how I would find my classes, and if I would see my big sister during the day. She squeezed my shoulder and reassured me that there would be plenty of people there to help me find my way around. She told me not to worry, that I would make friends.

Being the new person in school is not easy. You walk into an unfamiliar environment and though you let your eyes scan the room, you know there will not be a single familiar face to pull you into conversation. Socially school did not get off to a good start. I found myself sticking out sorely from the beginning. When I talked, I didn't sound the way I was, as a black girl, supposed to sound, and everyone did not neglect to inform me of this fact. The black kids told me that I talked like a white girl. They weren't mean about the comments, they were said with an undercurrent of humor running through them, but I felt lonely and confused. This was not an accusation I was familiar with. So when words like "oreo" were directed at me, I looked away in frustration. It didn't take me long to understand what they meant. I wanted to unleash my irritation on them. I was not talking like a white girl. I was talking exactly like I had always been talking. I was talking like me. I hung my head in unexpressed frustration. I did not have the energy to debate the validity of my blackness. And then came the questions, where was I from, what about the lions, what about the starving children, did I live in a hut, did I carry fruit on the top of my head. Apparently in America, Africa is epitomized by starving children and lions in your backyard. I rolled my eyes in annoyance.

In America the word immigrant, a word I had not needed to incorporate into my vocabulary until this point, is like strapping a back pack full of bricks onto your shoulders. It means that in the eyes of the government you are just a series of numbers and letters, mine starting with letter A. It is very impersonal, but it helps them keep track of your comings and goings, and for years my goings were limited by my status. It means that even when you have no reasons to worry, you worry anyway because acceptance shifts depending on which candidate is in power, and you can never be quite sure what side of the line you fall on. You are invisible and visible simultaneously, seen perhaps in the ways you wish you could be unseen and vice versa. It means that some are welcoming and others want you to return directly from where you came from. That for some, just by being, you are a threat. It was new to me. I was resentful but I did not know who to blame. I had taken belonging to a nation for granted, I realized. But no one told me that I would be spending the next years of my life flinching at words such as "deportation," so how could I have known?

Needless to say, Auntie was wrong, I did not make friends immediately. It did not concern me. I had other things on my mind at the time. We weren't at that school long, but I learned some significant lessons. I learned that eventually, once the shock wears off, children will stop asking you why you sound the way you do, and that they will make room for you within their circles, as long as you are sincere. I also learned that I was good at school. I learned and retained new information with ease. At school I was bold, I was useful and competent, and I let myself feel it. I let myself soak in the gold stars and the accolades, let myself stand straight and spell the hard words at the front of the class. I beamed at my test scores, a foreign sense of pride sitting inside my chest. That was my first education in the power of those small letters printed on the lines of progress reports and report cards. I began to visualize those grades as a means to an end. It was not necessarily about passion or enjoyment. School was practical, a big sign above the door of my life that read EXIT in flashing letters. I liked the look of it so I focused myself. I asked Auntie at nighttime what one had to do to get into the gifted program. I asked her about how one gets into college. And especially, I asked her about this word I had started hearing: scholarship. I needed one of those, so I added it to my to-do list. I often wondered which version of myself was the real one. If both parts met each other on the side of the road, they would not smile in recognition, they did not know each other at all. I wondered if this girl, whose head was inclined upward, chin high, who completed assignments with confidence and ease was me. Or was I the girl who, at home, flinched every time the air shifted, whose heart hammered with untamable vigilance at the sound of a door opening or a floorboard creaking. I did not know.

At the house the tension between Auntie and Mum kept barreling toward its eventual tipping point. I walked in from the bus one afternoon and I knew that exact tipping point had arrived. Mum was walking briskly around the house, pausing in the living room so that she and Auntie could raise their voices at one another. I still could not figure out the details of what they were arguing about. I looked at my sisters and we used our feet to match Mum's brisk pace and closed ourselves inside our small bedroom. This was not the day to find yourself in the way.

It happened quickly after that. One day we were sitting in our room in one home, and another we were packing up our things while trying to dodge her anger, and one more day and we were driving away to a new home, to a new school, to another new life. It happened just like that. No explanations and no warnings. I hardly even remember saying goodbye. It all felt like a game, the worst kind of deja vu. I'm sure I hugged Auntie with tremors in my body, no tears because we were under scrutiny. I'm sure she promised we would see each other soon, that we could come and spend the night and clean crawfish in the kitchen sink again. She likely even whispered into my ear that I should not worry before drawing back and flashing me her wide smile. I was not foolish enough to believe her and it turns out I was justified. I did not see her again for six years. I felt exhausted. How many new beginnings must a person endure in the span of one lifetime? More than I imagined, apparently.

DOVE

Frail little frightened dove
    Fragile efforts—not enough
    Slowly falling.
    Failing.
    Falling.
    Weary, weeping, always longing.

    Faulty little fractured dove
    Fleeting solace—overcome
    Dimly flying.
    Flitting.
    Flying.
    Wailing, weeping, always pining.

    Fickle little fallen dove
    Famished spirit—ever crushed
    Gently fading.
    Fainting.
    Fading.
    Wanting, weeping, always waiting.

I would like to pause here because the next part of the story is grim. Did you scoff? Honestly I did. I understand that it has likely felt grim already. What I mean is that, the worst part is still ahead. Don't let this discourage you from continuing, the light does come. Eventually.

I would like to pause here because in the next part I will describe her in the fullness of her monstrosity. We will move into the townhouse I still have dreams about and everything will go up a notch. I will tell you what happened and what did not happen and you will, as I did, hate her. So I would like to pause here to remind you that she is human.

I am not making excuses.

But I would like you to remember what this person had endured up to this point. The ways that her life had shifted so entirely. I just want you to remember that the man that she loved had chosen other things over her, even though bullets had flown into her body, ripping at her flesh, on his behalf. I would like to petition you to remember that she had almost died, that her body would never be the same after that, and that when it rained and her knees hurt, she would have to be reminded of lying on the veranda in her own blood trying not to die. That her life metamorphosed from luxury into scraping by with three children and no help from the man who had helped her conceive them. That her pride was being crushed underneath the weight of having to accept handouts from church members, like backwards Cinderella. I would like to pause here to remind you that she is human.

You will still hate her, as I did for a long time, but maybe a little bit less.

I am in two minds about the brown townhome on Lemonwood Trail. On one hand that place taught me I was formidable. It taught me that my resilience was my biggest weapon. That even as she tried to push my head underneath the ground, I would find new ways to stand up and keep limping along. Don't misunderstand me. If giving up had been an option I would have happily selected it. I even allowed myself a few pit stops along the way, laying down and entertaining giving up and letting life win, but I always got back up. We are wired for survival, as I have said, and in my mind, if I had to be alive, then I might as well do so to the best of my ability. I was focused and when I am focused, I am stubborn and unrelenting, you can ask my friends today. I furnished my imaginary future with the safety and stability I could not yet have. I pictured myself in a home all alone, a controlled environment wherein I was in charge. There I would sleep through the night. In that world I'd have a stable and predictable job. I'd walk in the door and cherish the stillness and serenity. And most of all, in that place to come, I would not need or depend on anyone. It was an intoxicating thought. My resilience was also, naturally, my greatest downfall. She did not like my silent power and it forced her to re evaluate her approach to maintaining control. She learned to exploit my softness, that foolish part of me that was desperate for her love. To tease it out of hiding and then use her foot to pin it to the floor.

But let me not rush ahead.

The exterior was not beautiful. The brown-green panels were frayed and warped, aged over humid summers and indecisive winters. Small wood fences lined the small spaces between our driveway and our neighbors on either side. I didn't understand the utility of this tiny fence, seeing that we shared a wall with our neighbors. I could at times hear the small dog of our right side neighbor yapping away, presumably at a squirrel perched on their deck, or maybe at the television. The condo was built so that an awning jutted out beyond the border of the house with a little covered space masquerading as a garage. Mum had the good sense not to park her car under there, deciding that the chances of that shabby roof collapsing outweighed the odds of any severely inclement weather. In the corner, the land-lord had left his old grill and a tangle of used tools. The place was plain and uninviting, the entire scene a muddy wash of grays and browns. Our landlord had kindly planted one tree at the edge of our driveway, gangly and with small leaves when we moved in, but by spring, that Dogwood sprouted to life, clothing itself in pungent white beauty. My allergies also sprouted to life, but I appreciated the gesture.

The interior of the house was small and generic. A small foyer branched off into an office which backed up into a kitchen. It always felt like a shame, the size of that kitchen. It mocked the kind of chef Mum was and it made my eyes sting in remembrance of former things. The kitchen connected to a small dining room, one whole wall constructed of mirrors, like in a dance studio. Maybe whoever built this place knew that we would be grateful to always be able to see what was coming behind us. Off to the side, a small living room housed a small couch and a television. Underneath Mum stored our photo albums and her collection of CDs. Her taste in music was, in my opinion, impeccable. When she was at work, I'd listen to Sade, or maybe Barry White, while I laid on my belly flipping through photos of the home and life I longed so desperately to return to.

The narrow stairs in the space between the front door and the living room lead to the three bedrooms at the top of the house. Big sister was allowed her own room while I was forced to share with baby sister. I loved her but she annoyed me, always whining and running off to use her sweet round face to tell Mum stories that did not have favorable outcomes. That was what little kids did, I know, but she did not yet understand that, in our house, we did not invite Mum into our business unnecessarily. She learned eventually. I did not complain about having to share with her. It could have been worse. Mum's room sat at the end of the hallway, her own semi private world. A world that, if possible, you did not want to be invited into.

We would, on those rainy weekend days, get trapped inside there. She'd entice us in and pat her bed urging us to sit in a small circle around her. She'd pull out a deck of cards and a bag of jelly beans. I'd take in her smile and the grief would envelope me anew. Imagine if she smiled like that all the time. Imagine if she stayed soft. I saw the untapped maternal potential in her in those moments and it left my knees wobbly with longing. We listened as she instructed us on the numerical value of each different color. Purple would be worth $5, green $2, orange $1 and so on.We'd pile on her bed and sit cross legged and gamble the time away, laughing as we snuck candy into our mouths in between rounds. My usual vigilance would soften as my body hummed from sugar intoxication. I felt in part like I was betraying myself by allowing myself to have a good time. I wish good and evil were mutually exclusive. I wish she did not house both in her wide frame. It complicated things. It intensified the devastation when, after winning the round, her hand suddenly reached for you, starting out as a stroke on the cheek before turning suddenly into a pull of the lip, her slender finger hooking inside the mouth followed directly by an insult, perhaps one of her favorites,

"Look at your fat face, Miss Piggy," chased by a succession of crude snorts.

She was still smiling as she said it, but it was no longer warm, the previous moments interrupted like a loud snap of the fingers in the middle of a quiet room. It was repeated experiences like this that twisted enjoyment into something I could not tolerate easily. I did not like the loss of control associated with pleasure. And it never seemed to come without a price. I climbed off her bed humiliated. I did not run because I was not in the mood to provoke her further. I did not whimper because I knew it was entirely pointless. I walked out slowly, the effort of each step feeling suddenly monumental, the weight of longing to be beautiful and adored sitting like a mountain on the chest. You would think the body would just stop producing the tears altogether. That after a while your system becomes depleted and there is nothing left. But it was never like that for me. The reason I cried changed, of course, at first it was out of hope that someone would come and pick me up from where I sat crouched in a half circle, but when that didn't work, I just cried to maintain some of my softness. For later years.

ON THE FARM in Africa we had people who cleaned our house and prepared our food. They did our laundry and pinned our clothes on lines tied between two poles to dry in the hot, moisture-less heat. They tidied our dishes and mopped the black and white kitchen tile. Mum cooked and baked because she enjoyed it. Dad roasted his chickens because it relieved the stress that had built up inside his body. My sisters and I occasionally stood by the hot stove observing this worker or that as they stirred maize flour into boiling water, watching it slowly harden as they moved their wrists in circles vigorously. We observed out of curiosity but not obligation. Our relatives teased Mum, telling her we were spoiled, that we should learn how to cook the traditional dishes and speak the language. But at the time, we did not have need for either of those skills.

Lemonwood Trail was an awakening for each of us. The leap from luxury to poverty was broad and when we landed on the other side our knees buckled underneath us from the impact. Mum had always worked in the financial world, holding positions that put her ability to adapt and solve problems to good use. But in America, her training and skills seemed to become almost obsolete. That is the plight of many immigrants, I have learned, that training obtained elsewhere does not carry over very well into America. I pitied her. I could see the way the shame seemed to weigh her shoulders down. The way the unspoken resentment caused her hair to start thinning at the edges. I could tell by the way the house was never devoid of bottles of gin or packs of cigarettes hidden underneath her mattress. She lost the pride with which she carried herself through the world. The Americans could not tell this, she still appeared proud outside the doors of the household, but inside she moved like a hollowed shell of her former self. I did not think it possible for me to miss the old version of her. But I was wrong.

I pitied myself too, because as she struggled to provide for us, working eight hours every day as a teller at the local bank, her remaining patience atrophied quickly. The skills that had once not been necessary became expected. I understood that and I was willing, if not eager, to help. The only problem was her unwillingness to teach us gently. We were thrust into this new world and expected to know how to cook and clean up to her, as always unachievable, expectations. We learned quickly after weeks of suffering under the medley of her insults and the beatings that followed.

IN SOME WAYS we were utterly normal. Our lives seemed to mimic the rhythms of other children, especially on paper. During the week we woke ourselves up in the morning, taking turns in our small bathroom, moving in and out of our bedrooms like a well oiled machine. I brushed baby sister's hair while she screamed about the pain caused by the brush catching in her constant cornucopia of knots. I shook big sister awake, reminding her of the consequences of missing the bus. I twisted my own braids into a bun on the top of my head, threw a shirt over my head and descended the stairs where Mum waited. She looked us up and down, poking here or there, smoothing this or that, until she was satisfied. We were still in the business of making an impression. Our appearance reflected on her and she was determined that, even with our drop in socioeconomic status, we would still move through the world with the sensibilities befitting our former lives.

On the weekdays, school and homework were our first priority. By the time Lemonwood was home, I was in the middle of seventh grade, big sister was in eighth and baby sister was in first grade. Mum's expectations about school were unrealistic but clear. In fact, excuse me while I take a moment to tip my hat to her in thanks because my work ethic was birthed at the dining room table of that townhouse. I knew that as soon as I walked into the house, I was expected to sit down and get to work. I rarely even paused for a sip of water. When Mum walked down the stairs, she expected your bottom to be pressed into the chair and your eyes to be focused. When I was through, I checked over everything meticulously, and only then did I allow myself a respite for the day. It was a routine fueled visibly by fear and invisibly by an empowering knowledge that education was the only paper power I had left. I had packed my determination in my suitcase as we traveled away from Auntie's house. I continued to push myself academically, surprising myself by achieving more than I had anticipated. I was not at the new school long before a letter was shoved into my hand, informing me that I would be tested for the Gifted Program. I beamed internally, the fruit of my striving bound tightly in my fist. Mum did not display any outward pride, but for once, I hardly registered the sting. Her affection in this case was not a priority of mine.

Big sister, on the other hand, occupied the school hours in a much different fashion. She was popular and beautiful, and as always, the boys were always enticed by her charm and charisma. Instead of focusing in class, she snuck sappy love notes and forbidden kisses (I don't blame her, her boyfriend was handsome and I often found myself wishing he would kiss me instead of her). She snuck downstairs in the middle of the night to send messages back and forth on instant messenger. In the afternoon while Mum was still at work, she'd pull the phone into the downstairs bathroom and talk to whichever boy was hers at the moment. I'd bang my fist on the door and when she opened, look at her in warning. If report cards were based on social standing she would have been at the top of her class. But they are not and I knew those afternoon phone calls would eventually catch up to her in the worst way possible. I was right of course, and when the end of the quarter came, the sight of her report card was devastating. It stared back at me with letters I didn't even know were possible to achieve. I was enraged. I looked at her with a mixture of empathy and disgust. I loved her, but at times I experienced big sister's antics like some sort of force pulling me backward into the very places I was working so hard to escape. For me those report card days were one of the few moments when I allowed my constant fear to take a rest. I knew I was safe. Would Mum comment on that one 89 that should have been a 90? Sure. But I could manage that. What I knew none of us could manage was what would happen if Mum caught sight of those letters on big sister's papers. Part of me wanted to let her climb out of this mess on her own. It wasn't my problem. But as I said, in the business of staying alive, I could not only worry about myself. Her problems were always my problems as well. That is why when she begged me to let her sign the back of the envelope we had to return to school, I paused to let myself consider it. I sat there doing math equations, adding the sum of the parts of this potential path and others. Maybe part of me knew that we would get caught, but I still had to choose, and seeing the fear inside my sister causing lines all over her face? I knew I had to say yes. So I did.

It was a good choice for a while. Mum asked us where our report cards were but since neither of us seemed to have received one, it was easy for her to believe that they were delayed. Actually, as I write that sentence, I suddenly wonder if she knew all along that we were lying and was just waiting to have the proof firmly planted in her hands. I would not put it past her. We hadn't thought the entire plan through. Back then, your report card was sent home in the same envelope each time, meaning that every signature over the entire year was visible on lines stacked up against each other on the backside. As it happens, fate also ensured that we would be daughters to a mother whose signature was so complex, the twists and turns and hoops of the first letter alone were confounding. We did our best, but our choice was plainly visible.

I spent so many days on the bus trying to get my insides to stop clamoring up my throat. I despised going home. I had to hang up my self confidence like a jacket at the end of every school day, and outfit myself in that heavy cloak of fear and shame I was so weary from carrying on my back. As soon as the last bell rang, I'd find myself dragging my feet to wait for the bus in such a state of disquietude. I'd lean my head against the window, my middle school classmates giggling and flirting and then me, palms already sweating uncomfortably. It often felt hard to breathe, as if some cord of flesh was being tightened around my neck. I wanted to close my eyes and disappear.

That day was no different. I rode home in silence, insides flailing about, report card in my hands. I could have felt proud of how well I'd done, but as usual, I had to forego those positive feelings and focus my attention on what I imagined would happen next. I knew we couldn't lie again, could not pretend the report cards were late. I knew she would wonder, and perhaps this time, she would not have the patience to wait like a snake in a garden for our own foolish plan to backfire.

My sister and I sat on her bed talking in whispers. I was terrified, and to make matters worse, big sister's grades had not improved. I felt angry and betrayed. I had agreed to this to protect her, so that she would have time to focus and raise her grades. I wanted to shake her. The feeling that this had been for nothing landed like a stone in the very bottom of me with a thud and I wanted to scream at her. Why must she always play with fire? I hated her for it but I didn't mention it. There were already enough variables at play. I just held her hand while we reassured each other it would be alright, maybe she wouldn't notice the forged signature and big sister's poor grades would be all we had to contend with.

After we placed the report cards on the edge of mum's bed, we just sat in silence waiting. She called big sister in first. I felt that urge to bolt out of our front door and run and run and run and never look back. The tears were starting to rise and cause my vision to go blurry, but I instructed them to please wait until later.

Now that familiar crack, shoe, perhaps, or hand, ripple, tears. And then, my name floating calmly, yet distinctly down the corridor. I closed my eyes and took a breath, took a second to organize my insides, then went quickly, pushed open the door and found my sister crying at the foot of the bed, and her, that emotionless face, those empty eyes looking directly at me,

"Whose signature is this?" she asked, her slender finger pointing at my report card envelope. Another breath.

"Yours," I whispered. The slap came so quickly, I hardly registered her hand flying through the air. Again she asked, her voice still calm, "whose signature is this?"

"Yours," I said again, deciding to keep the story consistent.

Now fist on soft flesh, my body landing on the floor, followed by one bare footed kick to the gut. I wailed, hearing her narrating her next move, a phone call to the police to report us for forging her signature. I dragged myself up and begged her not to,

"I'm sorry, Mum, please, you do not have to call them" I whimpered, trying to stop her from making the call. It was my mistake, forgetting momentarily her hatred for the sound of a whimper.

Next, the phone receiver against my forehead.

"Shut up!"

And this time I did. I did. The phone rang out over the speaker phone, while my imagination went bouncing around in my head. I did not know what the consequences of forgery were but I imagined the worst. Would they take my big sister away? And what about me? I was undoubtedly an accomplice.

Seconds later baby sister shuffled cautiously into the room. She looked at my face and screamed so loudly, the operator, now on the phone, asked Mum what that was. She ran to the television and turned it up, telling them it was just the tv. I touched the place where the phone receiver had connected with my temple, brought my palms down to have a look: blood, sticky and wet, covering my hands.

I didn't react audibly. I swallowed down the emotion seizing up in my throat and walked slowly into the hallway bathroom. Do you know what it takes to swallow down panic? What it takes to see yourself covered in blood and ask the body not to react? To not make a sound? It is in itself a form of twisted torture. I glanced up at my reflection. Took in those little rivers of blood trickling down my face, around my eyelid. I didn't want to wash it off. I wanted the police to come and I wanted them to see. I contemplated it seriously for just a moment.

But I was not stupid. Nor was I brave.

I wiped my face gently, red blood mixing with clear tears. When I walked out of the bathroom, she was there at the door. Her cold stare was punctuating every word as she said,

"Change your shirt before they get here."

I did.

When the police came, two men with their intense gazes and unmovable demeanors, mom recited the story of what we'd done, conveniently leaving out her own violent reaction. As the police gave big sister and I a stern talking to, a warning about the consequences of such acts, I was there pleading with my eyes. I wanted them to pay attention, to read between the lines, to notice the way the house was reeking of blood and unsafety. But they didn't notice and instead piled themselves back into their car and drove away. The next day, the guidance counselor called me into her office and asked me what happened to my head. I lied. It was easy. She sent me back to class with a hall pass. Presumably you are now wondering why I didn't tell the truth, didn't send a flare into the room and beg for help. I understand. But my life was not just my life, I could not just think of myself in this case. I had to weigh all the possible outcomes in my mind in an instant and decide if the truth was worth the risk. And it wasn't.

Not yet.

This was not the last time big sister's bad grades brought trouble back into the house. As I said she was preoccupied by her boyfriend and continued to perform badly academically. She weathered the beatings that resulted like a champion and somehow they did not move her into submission. I could not understand it, but then again, I had never been in love, as she said she was. Once, the following year, when she was in high school and so the first to get home at the end of the day, she snuck that very love of her life into the townhouse on Lemonwood Trail. Mum had interrupted them, she later relayed to me, caught them kissing on the old couch in the living room. I came home to big sister sitting in the downstairs half bathroom, her natural hair clipped unevenly, a punishment Mum knew would break her. My sister prided herself on her good looks (and so did everyone else. She was the "face of the family" and everyone remarked upon her beauty) and having her hair chopped off in chunks devastated her. She could manage the beating, the swollen lip and the soreness that lived in her body, but this? It was more than enough. She told me she would now be sleeping in the bathroom on the few blankets Mum had allowed her. Later that night, as I was completing my homework on the computer, Mum stormed down the stairs and into the bathroom, perhaps to bang her fists against big sister's body a few times. When she opened the door, big sister stood, waving one of the large kitchen knives in Mum's face. Mum just laughed, asking big sister what she intended to do. I wondered too. In the end it was nothing.

So, you see, we were not always good girls. Sometimes we made bad and very stupid choices. Sometimes Mum was entitled to her disappointment. She always took everything too far, that disappointment boiling up and over into an uncaged fury that never seemed to fit the crime, if there was a clear crime to begin with. I envied my friends who complained that their phones had been taken away or whined about not being able to go to the movies on the weekend.

On Friday nights I would only half sleep, terrified that Mum would wake first the next morning. We had learned the hard way that when she woke on Saturdays, when her thick feet landed on her bedside carpet and she stretched her hands upwards to clear the dreams from her system, we were expected to be somewhere in the house on our hands and knees. She had not informed us of this rule, so on one of our first Saturdays in the townhouse, we slept overlong, trying to catch up from late nights during the school week. It was her musky breath that first alerted me to her presence above my bed. And then her hand lost inside my long braids. A tug. A familiar ripple. A melody of words. It did not end there. That was the thing with Mum, once she got going, you paid for your mistake the entire day. While cleaning, a pot against your backside. While washing the dishes, an insult or ten. While cooking, a pull, a pinch, a twist of your skin. Just constant reminders of how worthless we were. Why do you think she did not just ask politely? I would have been happy to oblige. I was very agreeable as a child, but she failed to notice.

After that I spent those Friday nights flinching at any shift in the house. I sat upright when big sister went to the bathroom. I held my breath when baby sister turned over in the bed. As soon as the sun peaked its head over the horizon, I was wide awake. I watched the minutes flip over on the digital clock. I let my sisters sleep, an unspoken understanding between us that I would keep watch. And then, at six twenty nine on the dot, I reached over, preemptively turned off the alarm and shook them awake.

We went to work immediately. We gathered our laundry for the upcoming afternoon trip to the coin laundry down the street. We cleaned the bathrooms and the kitchen until the appliances sparkled, making sure to cover the nooks that she checked meticulously. We scowled at and shoved each other in warning as we checked over each others work. Downstairs we swept the floors and spot cleaned the carpets with Resolve, making sure the surface was clear of any obvious marks. We pulled all the pictures off the wooden side tables so we could remove the dust that had accumulated over the week.

When we heard her stirring upstairs, we scattered to separate parts of the house. She did not like us working together, often insulting us for being so incompetent we could not complete tasks independently. She walked down stairs, her large breasts bouncing in her oversized t-shirt. She had a casual air about her, as if embracing Saturday cheerfully. A stranger might even have smiled and called out in greeting. But we were not strangers. You had only to look closer to see that her eyes were scanning the place, zooming in and out of corners, a detective looking for blood. It didn't take much to upend any hope of a peaceful morning. I once missed a small corner of the kitchen counter. She called me in as she was brewing her daily cup of English black tea. She did not speak, only pointed at the counter. I squinted my eyes, willing them to focus on the area she was pointing at. I could barely see the few specks of sugar that were apparently littered along the edge. I confess I wondered if she put the sugar there herself, but I can't be sure. She launched her empty tea cup straight for my head as if launching an axe at a target. I managed to dodge the cup but the teaspoon caught me in the head, a quick slice before tumbling to the floor. I still have the cut right at the base of my hair-line where my hair refuses to grow back.

Saturdays stretched on with remarkable slowness. After we finished cleaning to her satisfaction, we loaded ourselves into the old tan minivan she had haggled from some used cars salesman. We tucked our laundry into the boot of that car nervously. Then big sister and I fought over who would ride in the front seat. We were not like other children, racing each other to the passenger side or screaming out 'shot gun' and smirking with pride. The front seat was not a place we wanted to find ourselves. Don't misunderstand me, the back seat was only marginally better, Mum's hands seemed capable of growing long enough to reach behind and catch the skin of your shin under her fingernails if necessary. But at least in the back you could sink into the guise of peace for just a moment. When it was my turn upfront, I'd sit beside her with my breath held, trying my best not to look uncomfortable or stiff. She was perceptive about such things and if she caught you looking afraid she would give you even more of a reason to be.

The coin laundry fascinated me the first time we walked in. I liked the dirty rows of washers and dryers lined up against each wall. I liked the sound the machine made as I fitted four quarters into the receiver, pushed, and watched as the money disappeared into the washer's invisible belly. I liked the circular and hypnotic movement of our clothes spinning inside of the dryer, round and round and round. I like the rhythm of the place and I especially liked the people. The coin laundry was a unique conflation of cultures, ethnicities, races and more. People spoke loudly over the hum of the machines and it created a medley of different languages. As the day wore on, children and adults unpacked their lunches and all the smells danced together in pungent harmony. Mum would bring plastic bags packed with tupperware filled with her goat curry. She'd trade them for flaky samosas or red tinted jollof rice. I liked the feeling that inside the overheated laundromat, the playing field was evened out. We were all just people in need of clean clothes. Perhaps I was just heart sick for the way the intermingling of culture reminded me of our boarding school days.

In America I was a pupil sitting at the feet of every new experience. Those Saturday morning laundry runs, for example, taught me that if even a little bit of bleach touches Mum's black panties for a second, they will turn a very unseemly color. The day I learned that lesson, I watched the interaction of the chemical against the fabric, the slow way the pigment transformed matched the way my insides were shifting in awareness of the error I had just made. I stuffed them into my pocket and excused myself to the bathroom where I pressed them into the trashcan underneath the used paper towels and whatever else. I told my sisters later as we sat at the edge of the couch taking turns ironing the stack of clean clothes we had brought back. They chuckled as I explained the way I used my bare hands to reach the bottom of the trashcan. I laughed as well, savoring our little circle of secrets. But then I grew serious and reminded them: I am telling you so that you do not make the same mistake as I did.

My favorite Saturdays were the ones where the sun sat blazing in the sky and Mum agreed to let us spend the afternoon swimming at the neighborhood pool. She never accompanied us, gratefully, choosing instead to retire early into her own hidden world. That small pool was an oasis. Somehow I felt untouchable there, though our little townhouse wasn't far away. At home I was always scared. I was scared to sleep, I was scared to eat, to laugh, to breathe or to cry. I was scared to use the bathroom, often willing my bowels to empty a little faster lest I linger too long and the door flung open. You did not want to be caught naked by Mum. There are certain places I did not ever want her hands to travel again. What I am saying is that at home I was scared to exist. You never knew when or what could bring hands or objects or words in contact with your body. But there in that rectangular pool with it's clear chlorine scented water, I felt free. We laughed. We resurrected those childhood pretend games of mermaids and sea urchins. We held our breaths and competed to see who could survive without air the longest. We did handstands and backflips in endless succession. For a few hours, we were just three children, turning shades darker underneath the hot Atlanta sun. Nothing more, nothing less. It was like magic.

ONCE

Was I your baby, once?
    Before I lay perfectly still
    underneath the weight of your body
    The same body that brought me to life
    In a time of trouble
    Your blood, my very same blood
    Spilled blood
    On the crisp white sheets
    You turned to your side and went to sleep
    But me
    Still pinned down by something invisible
    The weight of being
    Damaged

Yet I will not forget you.
    Forget.
    Forgotten.
    There in the silent darkness.
    Heart pounding in the imposed stillness of the aftermath
    Me alone, you sleeping peacefully
    Tears dancing slowly down my face
    A cistern dying to break
    Grieving whatever died that day
    Never to return
    My throat raw with everything left unsaid
    The screams yet unspoken

Was i your baby, then?
    Your body invigorated
    Mine depleted
    Defeated
    As was always the way.

MARJIE MONRO

Eyes toward the door
   The unbroken part of me longing for
   Some phantom figure to appear
   Exhume the innocence in me
   Hold it fiercely
   But the footsteps never came.
   They never came.
   And in the rancid darkness
   The only sound was you
   Moaning while you slept.

It did not take long for Mum to find us a church to attend on our side of town. Unlike Auntie's, her choice was a Baptist church that was large enough to occupy the whole block of the street it sat on. The services felt stale in comparison, the large choir trumpeting out hymns that I found pulseless. No one raised their hands, and the few ladies in the back who decided to clap to the rhythm of the music earned a few critical looks from neighboring members. When the old pastor finally moseyed up onto the stage, he sporadically stomped his foot down onto the red carpet. I could never tell if he did so out of passion, or because even he knew that half the crowd was dozing off. At church Mum was a celebrity. She joined the choir and participated faithfully in Sunday School and Wednesday evening Bible Study. On Sundays she walked down to the altar during the invitation and knelt down to pray. Sometimes she held our hands and we knelt beside her. I did not pray. I watched her and wondered what her lips were moving so furiously about. She seemed so genuine, the usual scowl of her brow now softened into something more tender and passionate. In those moments the lines between real and pretend seemed to blur together leaving me confused. Who are you, I often wanted to whisper across at her, but I never did. On Wednesdays we ate as a family in the Fellowship Hall before we split off to our respective activities. Those dinners in the Fellowship Hall make my skin feel as if there are ants crawling against its surface. Eating under her scrutiny felt a like an entire punishment in itself. There was a mathematics to eating that I could never master. We could not eat too little, or we would be wasting the money she had paid for our meal, but eat too much and that created an entirely different problem. God the tears have sprung into my eyes as I have typed that sentence. It is because I can picture with such vividness the completeness of that scene. On the outside we are just a family having dinner together. Three girls seated together with a mother who is adored by everyone passing by. No one could see the mental gymnastics occurring inside my brain. No one was registering how I was calculating each bite of food as it was traveling from plate to fork to mouth. I still have a complicated relationship with food today. There are times I eat too much, fearful of not having enough and there are times when I do not eat at all, perhaps punishing myself or maybe simply forgetting to register hunger as a meaningful cue.

At church, the only stories anyone knew about Lemonwood Trail were the ones Mum sowed into the ears of pastors or friends. She spun them carefully to turn us into monsters, children who never listened or who were ungrateful for the sacrifices she was constantly making. I resented the talkings to we continued to get, whether from a friend of hers or from the outreach pastor, who also happened to be my best friend's father. He would pull us into his office and with the door closed, educate us on obedience and 'honoring your father and mother.' I nodded my head dutifully, the entire time trying desperately to figure out whether it was truly possible for everyone to be so entirely hypnotized by Mum or whether everyone was just too terrified to challenge her. Weren't these people meant to have a sense of discernment? How then were we the ones sitting across from this man as he handed us books to read and accused us subtly of submitting to darkness, or of being demon possessed? As he continued to remind us about the fruits of the spirit, I tilted my head down. He would have believed it was an action performed out of remorse, but it was not about remorse. It was about fury.

One time in particular, he scolded us for not being more grateful, for not recognizing the sacrifices that Mum had made for us. He was trying to keep his tone even, but his pitch climbed higher and higher as he tried to make sure we were getting the point. As the words were leaving his mouth, my mind was playing the incident in question back on a loop:

IT BEGAN ON A SATURDAY. Mum had gone shopping for her Sunday school class the following morning. She came home and we rushed to the door to help her unload the groceries. Wait a second too long to meet her and there were consequences. We arranged the groceries neatly in the refrigerator and stacked in the cupboards with care and precision, making sure to maintain an efficient pace. When we were finished, she told us that she'd bought some cherries and that we were welcome to have some. Moments like the report card forgery were easy for the equations in my head: when you forge your mother's signature, she will draw blood, clear and very easy to remember. Other times I couldn't quite identify which step I'd made that tipped the scales. It sometimes felt she was taunting us, giving us permission only to punish us for it in the end.

Like you, I am now wondering what possessed me to dip my hand into that bag of ruby cherries and let myself have a few. I shake my head now, draw my lips tightly against my face, and cringe with a sense of foreboding. I should have known what icy territory we were venturing into. But they were only cherries, no?

We ate a handful each, hands and mouths sticky, spitting the pits into the air and at each other, giggling softly. We allowed ourselves this little moment of freedom to be sisters gathered around the table. We whispered and told little secrets, our own sweet game of paper pretend. Perhaps we remembered Africa as we did so, those sticky days when the warm rain was plinking on the roof like a song and our daddy was home. Those days when Mum locked herself in the bathroom with her cocktails and we sailed through the house, stopping where daddy watched television and snuck sips of his beer.

We threw the pits away, made sure everything was back in its place and went to bed innocently.

The next morning started out normally enough. I'd shaken both sisters awake not long after the sun stretched its arms out across the sky. It was Sunday and we knew well enough by now the consequences of being late for church. The expectations were unspoken but clear. Once Mum descended the stairs, those heeled feet of hers announcing her before she was visible, we had better have our bottoms halfway out of the dining room chairs and moving toward the door. I slipped on my Sunday dress. It was my favorite because in it I felt I was very nearly pretty. It was a bright turquoise with a bold floral print stretched across its surface. A thick border of black trimmed the v neck collar and then twisted around my developing bosom before wrapping around my waist in a bow I always asked big sister to tie neatly.

We were ready, as expected, when her bedroom door sighed open. I looked us all over one more time and nodded approvingly at how neat we looked. She looked at us the same way when she finally reached the main floor, sucked the air through her teeth and told baby sister to change her shoes. That was when she disappeared into the kitchen and began rummaging around, first for the fixings of her morning tea and then for something in the refrigerator. Sound was comforting, the rustle of plastic, the clinking of a spoon against her favorite glass mug. It was when the air got strangely silent that the three of us started shifting uncomfortably. Silence was never good. First the fridge door opening. And then nothing. I slid my gaze across at big sister and held it there. Our eyes were talking to each other while we were counting the excruciating seconds of nothing. Her eyes were asking mine what we had missed but I shrugged because I could not come up with anything.

AND THEN — my name floating out of Mum's mouth, around the corner, and into my ears.

I CLOSED MY EYES. Steadied myself. Asked my body to move though it did not want to.

I PUSHED my head into the narrow doorway of the kitchen. I looked up at her and waited, my mind already scanning the possibilities. We had cleaned the kitchen, not left any trash out, we were all ready for church, our clothes were clean and ironed,

"Who ate these cherries?"

I blinked, stunned that after all these years, she still managed to surprise me as she pulled new unseen variables out of wherever she stored them. Mum, you see, could turn anything into trouble.

"We did," I stuttered, and tentatively, "you said we could have some last night."

The remaining cherries went raining all over the kitchen and with them a demeaning shower of insults pouring out from her. Did you ever wonder what it was like to strip naked in front of your mother, your favorite dress now a crumpled pile on the floor, and be made to stand in front of the full length mirror as she pulls at your flesh, long nails clamping around your nipples, twisting and digging until you want to scream from the pain? Did you ever wonder what it feels like to then, while fully exposed, be compared to an animal, a greedy elephant, or perhaps a whale? Did you ever wonder how your insides feel like they are being crushed under the weight of that very same elephant, how you feel so degraded that all you want to do is hide, but you know you can't? You can't because if you reach for your clothes, if you reach for some shred of your dignity, you will invite another variable into the room and it's not worth the risk. Did you ever wonder what is like for your tears to be falling in rivers and for it not to matter?

I wish I did not know.

She told us to sit down at the table and marched back into the kitchen. She pulled out every pot we had and every bit of food in the refrigerator. She cooked it all, laid out her twisted feast before us and told us,

"Since all you do is eat like pigs, you cannot get up from this table until you eat everything in front of you."

She stood there waiting for us to move. When we didn't, she helped us get started by pushing chicken and potatoes against our mouths and past our teeth. She clogged our throats with green beans and nshima. We ate to satisfy her. We ate to avoid more pain. We ate because she told us to.

She left us there, went to the second service at church. I felt sick imagining her being doted on and praised while we sat at that dining table whispering about what to do now. I wondered if she patted herself on the back, enamored at the way she could create such demeaning punishments on a whim. Or perhaps she acted in reverse order, dreamed up the punishment and then found a way to implicate us. I do not know.

We sat there crying silently. I was crying because I was sad but inside I was also trying to regulate the part of me that was vibrating with rage. We weighed the options, knowing we needed to make a dent in this food before the tires of the mini van screeched to a halt in the driveway. We grabbed a trash bag and funneled handfuls of food into it, tied its impregnated belly tightly and shoved it into the top shelf of big sister's closet, hidden, or so we thought, behind our winter sweaters. We would deal with it later. Our bellies were aching. So were other parts of us.

We held our breaths when we heard her keys jingling outside the front door. We ground our teeth as the metal of the deadbolt twisted open. She strolled in. Her arms were weighed down with more groceries. I wanted to scream as I watched her wash the dishes and begin again, preparing more food to add to the table. When she walked up the stairs I stopped breathing. I felt the blood pulsing inside my eardrums. She went straight to my sister's closet. I didn't understand how she could have known. Perhaps she left her ears at home while she was at church, or one discerning eye? Perhaps God agreed that we were demon possessed and had given her a vision, I could not be sure. All I know is that she pulled the trash bags right out from behind those sweaters and brought them back down the stairs. She emptied the contents onto our plates, slop for her little piggies. I felt humiliated and ashamed. I wanted to kill her, cut off her hands as they landed against me, I wanted to shove her in front of the mirror and make her hate herself.

I wanted to lay down and never get up again. I just felt so tired.

We ate until she told us to clean up and go to bed.

That night I lay awake clutching my cramping stomach. After baby sister's breathing evened out and I was sure she was asleep, I climbed out of my own small bed and tiptoed across the hallway to big sister's room.

"It's me," I whispered as I twisted her door open. It is important to announce yourself so that you don't cause unnecessary surges in already elevated cortisol levels. I climbed in beside her and we faced each other and wept silently while our foreheads touched. There wasn't any reason to speak. Eventually I rolled onto my back and pressed my eyes shut, overcome with helplessness. I reached out and gave her hand a squeeze, rolled out of her bed and returned to mine.

The next morning we were awakened by the smells of chicken curry, pigs trotters and the rich beefy smell of oxtails. Ordinarily my mouth may have watered. I would have looked forward to using the Nshima to drag a winding trail through the meaty oxtail gravy. She was an amazing cook and some of these dishes were my favorites. But today I felt the nausea slithering up my esophagus. I swallowed it down to save time. We went downstairs and found another feast. Yesterday's leftovers touching hands with brand new dishes. I shook violently while I brought the first bite up to my lips.

When she left the house that day, we renegotiated the blueprint of yesterday's plan. Once again we filled a trash bag. This time with less food so that it was believable. Big sister hefted that bag against her shoulder and ran out the back door of our little townhouse, into the woods behind our neighborhood and shoved the food behind a tree. I wonder if she considered staying out there. I wonder if she had considered letting her feet keep going and carry her far away from this place. I would not have blamed her. I pressed my face against the glass of the side door and waited with my heart squeezed inside my chest. And then exhaled when I saw her face peak back around the corner and her feet moving her back toward home.

The rest of the day dragged its feet in slow motion. Somehow our plan had worked and when her keys shimmied into the deadbolt, she did not question us about the missing food, nor somehow intuit that it was hidden behind a decaying tree. We sat at that table for hours, picking at congealing gravy, cold meat and flaccid chicken skins.

I was silently wondering how long this would go on when the shrill of the phone disturbed the silence. It was Great Aunt calling from Africa. Mum begrudgingly walked down the stairs and tossed the phone onto the dining room table. I wanted to pick up the receiver and feel Great Aunt's voice envelope me like a hug. I wanted her to say she was sorry, that she had spoken to Mum and that things like this would not happen again. I wanted her to say she was coming to get us, that we could come and make a home beneath the mango trees and tickle Great Uncle's feet again after he finished working.

She said instead, "You know how she is."

And she was right as well, we did know how she was. But her answer didn't feel like enough. I was feeling so unprotected.

Great Aunt's next instructions were simple. All we had to do was beg Mum for forgiveness, admit that we were wrong, that we had been ungrateful. I felt my stomach turning over. I hated the feeling that we were all trapped inside a game that we had to keep on playing even though we knew we could never emerge as winners. But here, between staying seated at the table or begging for forgiveness, the mathematics seemed simple. We walked up the stairs, knocked on her door and got on our knees in front of her. I could smell the alcohol on her breath, the scent of cigarette smoke lingering in her knotted body wrap. I fought the urge to vomit on her perfectly polished toes. She was not quick to forgive. Our pleas of apology had to be repeated and punctuated with tears and admissions that cut our dignity into shreds. It wasn't difficult. This was not the first or last time I would find myself in this position in front of her. I often wondered what was going through her mind, how she could drink cocktails while knowing we were sitting right below her, humiliated and afraid. I wished I could embody her temporarily, just to know what sort of power it took for someone to remain so unmoving. How she could look down at us, her hands folded across her large and uneven breasts, and let the minutes rush forward. How she herself did not break down before us, lower herself to her knees and embrace us and plead for us to forgive her? I would have held her. I swear I would have held her. I would have soothed the heavy head of my mama and told her it was alright, that we could start again. How I longed for us to start again.

INFANCY

I had a dream that after all this time we'd finally meet.

We stood face to face, anchored in the wreckage of then, of now.

My heart beat wildly, yours not at all.

My heart's uneven thrum stirred the ashes of everything I'd pretended to bury, awakening some infant in the bottom of me, that cry now so ancient, rusty with need.

I watched you, curious to see if some phantom mother in you would finally soothe the forgotten baby in me.

Nothing.

And suddenly my eyes saw you differently, caged in by your own unsoothed grief.

I saw you flinch- just slightly- uncomfortable with the possibility of finally being seen in your entirety.

"Oh," my insides sighed and reached into the depths of you, dug through, until, there, so near the bottom, easy to miss--

A forgotten infant in you.

"Shhh, I've got you," said my heart to that little child, "I've got you."

She dismissed us with a nod, instructing us to clean up the mess on the table. I rose and dusted my knees off while walking out. I was one third relieved, one third devastated, one third disgusted. I could not identify whether the disgust was directed at her or at myself, or maybe it was a shared portion.

I locked myself inside the hall bathroom. I wept into my palms silently, repulsed by myself. I looked up at myself in the mirror. I pulled at myself, mocked myself, as I had seen her do so many times. It felt pathetic that I would demean myself in front of her in that manner, a mortifying act of self violation. It was as if parts of me were going to war with each other. One part shouted, "How could you give up your self respect so easily," while the other whispered, "What choice did I have?"

And one more part straining against the internal fragmentation to hold all of me together, to preserve some version of wholeness. It felt exhausting to carry on like this, hating myself for doing the very things that preserved my life in the end. I myself was an equation I could not seem to make sense of.

I wondered if she was looking at herself in the mirror on the other side of the wall, maybe smirking proudly at her reflection. Or maybe struggling to reconcile the mathematics of her own insides.

W hen I was in seventh grade, I had the seeming misfortune of being forced to take German to fulfill my language requirement. I had wanted to take Spanish, understanding even then that the language would have more future usefulness. I wasn't the only one who understood that, apparently, because the classes filled themselves quickly. I moved on to French, comforting myself with the fact that I had taken a few lessons as a child. I found the sound of the language melodious, and even though it would not be as practical as Spanish, it was a worthy opponent. When the guidance counselor told me that French was full too, I huffed and begged, unwilling to settle for the only available option: German. German, I had decided, would not enhance my eventual college applications the same way Spanish or French would. In the end I had no choice. I resigned myself to the language, telling myself I would take it for one year until something else opened up.

Af first I found myself sitting in class with my lips pursed together in annoyance. We learned songs to keep track of the letters of the alphabet and rhymes that reminded us of the rules of conjugation. I didn't want to be there. My teacher noticed my disinterest and pulled me aside at the end of one class. She asked me about my attitude and I told her the truth: this had not been my preference. It was then that she began telling me stories about her childhood in Germany, about the reasons that keeping the language alive was so personal for her. Despite my efforts, it warmed me slightly. I liked the way she talked to me like an adult. I liked that when I answered her questions she wanted to know more. It made me feel visible in a way that interested me.

That was the first of many conversations shared at the end of class or during lunch. She asked me about home and how it is that I came to be in this country. I felt safe. The twinness of our immigration stories helped me not feel so alone. She snuck in anecdotes about her difficult relationship with her mother and after a while I began to wonder if my mind was see through. I looked at her and it was as if the future I imagined for myself had manifested in front of me in tangible form. She had made it, journeyed through the darkness and emerged on the other side, not just alive, but still full of compassion and warmth. When one day she asked me if I wanted to babysit her children one Friday night, I wanted to scream "yes!" excitedly. I wanted nothing more than to spend a few hours inhabiting someone else's life. A few hours to escape.

"I'm not sure," I told her, already anticipating Mum's response and refusal.

I spent the rest of the day doing equations inside of my head. I was adding and removing variables over and over again trying to land on the formula that might result in a nod of approval. That night, I waited until the smell of cigarette smoke started sneaking out from under her door, I waited until she had collected her tonic water from the refrigerator, and then I tapped my knuckles against her bedroom door. I took a deep breath as she gave me permission to enter, taking one more second to remind myself of the equation I had landed on by the end of the day. It was simple: maintain a level tone, do not betray any excitement, and most importantly, offer her the money that would be earned by the end of the night. It was worth a try.

After Mum agreed I exited her room in a state of euphoria. That excitement carried me through the week and when the day finally came, I climbed into my teacher's minivan as she drove us the short distance to her house. I felt shy as she introduced me to her husband and two children, embarrassed as if I was trespassing. But as her children pulled at my hands and invited me into their playroom, I felt myself relax slightly. It surprised me when, instead of getting ready and immediately leaving me to my role as babysitter, my teacher invited me to sit across from her in the living room and asked me about home and about Mum. I was reluctant to tell her, aware of the trouble she could make if my stories left the small space we inhabited. By then I was aware of how the police or the department of children's services seemed either to do nothing or if they did intervene and then leave, make things worse. I told her how the police had come and how they had left. I hinted at the consequence of such incidences. I made her promise that if I let her inside of my world, she would not tell anyone. It was a lot to ask, I know. I could see the conflict playing itself out on the surface of her face. it was a battle waged between her ethical obligations as a teacher and her desire to offer me a safe place in which I could deposit all of my pain. I would not have faulted her if she had chosen the former, but she will forever have my gratitude that in that moment she stuck her pinky finger out and promised me that my secrets would remain with her. And so I told her. Not everything, but enough. I told her that. I told her how not long before, the school counselor having suspected abuse had made a report and how children's services had showed up at the school and started prodding me for information. I told her how the police had come and how they had left. I hinted at the consequence of such incidences

After that we were careful to maintain an appropriate distance at school. She never treated me with favoritism and perhaps graded my papers with more keen eyes. At the end of the week, I spent at least one evening at her house herding her energetic children to the dinner table or chasing them outside. Sometimes she would pick me up early to babysit, bringing with her a trunk half full of groceries to help Mum. I always remained cool as she and Mum exchanged niceties. I called her by her formal name as if we were at school and did not look her in the eyes, afraid my affection for her would be apparent. When we got into the car, she gave my shoulder a squeeze, and off my mouth went, filling the entire drive to her house with stories and fears and dreams. At the end of the night she would pay me for the hours I spent with her children. I always felt guilty accepting it. The gift of a safe haven felt like compensation enough. I told her once but we both knew that if I did not have cash to place on Mum's dresser at the end of the night, all of this safety would disintegrate. We discovered we attended the same church on Sundays, which thrilled me. It provided a legitimate reason why it made more sense for me to spend the night in her home on Saturdays and join Mum and the girls at church the following morning. I felt lucky and relieved. It is amazing how much more a person can weather when they are afforded one slice of safety on which to lean on.

It went on like this through the entire school year and into the first signs of summertime. When my birthday arrived, German teacher invited the entire family to spend the day at the large aquarium a few hours outside of town. Mum agreed. All of us, with the exception of big sister, who was forced to stay home and iron basketfuls of clothing, an ongoing punishment from Mum's discovery of her secret AIM messages, loaded into the car and drove North to the aquarium. Looking back I can see in slow motion the way things had started to go wrong from the very beginning. It was in the way teacher's children held my hands and how they had insisted I ride in the back with them. It was in the way teacher kissed my cheek as she handed me my birthday gift and how her first name slipped out of my lips as we walked around the aquarium. It was in the way, distracted, I failed to include baby sister more. In my excitement I had let my vigilance slip.

The day itself went okay. As I have said, Mum could make a profession out of the way she was able to play pretend and maintain her composure.We wandered around the aquarium in a group, us children pointing and staring wide eyed as the animals glided around us and overhead. We stuck our hands into cool water to feel the slick backs of stingray and watched as jelly fish danced behind colored panes of glass. I laughed, I sank my weight into German teacher's shoulder, I spun her kids around.

I forgot myself.

It wasn't until much later, after we had made the drive back to Atlanta, after we arrived back at the house and walked in the door, that I realized things were amiss. I walked in and found big sister behind the ironing board where we had left her. I sat down beside her and started telling her about the day and whispering to her that I wish she had been there. Mum went into the kitchen and began rummaging through the refrigerator, looking for dinner. She stuck her head into the living room and asked me if I wanted to ride with her to pick up some chicken wings. I'm not sure what possessed me, because instead of simply agreeing as I usually would, I said absently,

"I'm tired, would it be okay if I stayed?"

I know what you are thinking. You do not have to tell me what an error I had just made. I saw it in the look she gave me and in the way her lips curled slightly at the edges. She launched into a narrative about how I did not want to spend time with her. I tried to recover the situation quickly, launching into my own defense about just being tired and apologizing repeatedly. Inside I was scolding myself for my stupidity. Eventually she acquiesced and allowed me to reconsider her offer. Big sister gave my thigh a squeeze as I rose from the couch beside her, in comfort or perhaps in warning.

Mum was silent on the drive to the wing place adjacent to the run down gas station. I sat very still in the seat beside her. I was replaying what had just transpired and readying myself. I knew it was not over. I had gotten by far too easily. I hated the ramp up time, those minutes where it was clear she was stewing and perhaps contemplating her next move. It is a form of mental torture that is hard to articulate. The hairs on my neck were standing at attention and I could feel the fear becoming more and more amplified as the minutes wore on. I just wanted her to get on with it.

When we parked and entered the restaurant, she placed our order, telling the server it was to go because her daughter was too tired to sit in the restaurant. I wanted to argue but I clamped my mouth shut, no longer trusting myself to not just make things worse. As we sat across from each other in the lopsided booth, I watched as she shook her head and sucked air through her teeth, her mind clearly working steadily although she remained silent. I snuck a glance at the concealed kitchen praying that our order would not take long. She must have noticed my anxiety because that's when she snaked a hand out and pulled firmly on my ear. She began speaking quickly, an education in the way she had seen how much I loved being with teacher that afternoon, about how ungrateful I was, about how from this day forward she would not be my mother and did not want me to address her as such. She wanted me to know that I should not walk beside her or sit beside her, that I was not to accompany the family on certain outings. She told me I would no longer be allowed to babysit for teacher. My mind was fully awash with panic. I tried to soothe her with reassurances, to apologize, to perhaps cradle the jealousy that was erupting so obviously from inside her chest. I didn't know what else to do. The drive home was torture. I climbed into the back seat, obeying her request that I no longer sit beside her. Her mouth moved in insult the entire drive, her hands snaking back to grab at me and her nails scrapping at my skin. I wanted to ask her to pull over and please leave me on the side of the road. I'd had enough. When we arrived home, she parroted the story to big sister, as if big sister was now her ally. I tried to apologize again as she turned her weight toward me. I did not bother to run. I stood still as her hand caught inside the strands of my relaxed hair and as she used her hands against my body. I let her finish and collected myself from the floor, making a pile of the hair she had pulled off my head.

As I lay in bed that night I wondered how one day could feel like two separate and distinct lifetimes. I felt like I had started the day with so much and ended the day with nothing. I felt devastated at being cut off from the safety of teacher's home. I felt equally as devastated that I would have to spend the rest of the summer existing on the outskirts of my own family. It was as if the crumbs of Mum's affection that I had come to sustain myself on were stripped away. Mum was masterful in the way she made certain I experienced the fulness of emotional cutoff. It was surely a sinister game to her. I sat at home as the three of them went for ice cream or out for dinner. I was responsible for myself, tasked with keeping my clothes separate from theirs when we went to the laundromat. At the grocery store, Mum bought pieces of candy for my sisters while I walked behind them. I did not speak to her for weeks, was not permitted to look at her. When I tried, she either ignored me, or reminded me of the rules with a twist or tug of my ear or lip and a,

"What did I say?"

It was anguish. I am in part embarrassed to say how much I wanted her to speak to or acknowledge me. I am ashamed at how it hurt me to be so visibly relegated to the outside. I wish I had not loved her and been so desperate to belong to even this, the most dysfunctional of family units. But I was, and she knew it. She knew about my softness and my sensitivity and this punishment exploited those to their fulness. I would much rather her beat me till I bled than be left starving while the crumbs of emotional connection were withheld from me. It was that sensitivity that eventually, after weeks of separateness, carried my knuckles to her door. It was my softness that brought me down on my knees in front of her once more. I cannot articulate the humiliation one feels when they are forced to beg for the crumbs of love like some sort of animal. It is itself a severe form of self betrayal, to kneel still as you are first subjected to slurs before finally, *finally,* she agrees to be your mother again. The way as you leave her room you must again feel yourself fragment into two opposing parts.

Our need for connection is at once humanity's greatest strength and greatest weakness. I felt that firmly in my gut on that day.

AFTER ALL THESE YEARS

After all these years, you're still the place I come home to.

Against my will, my heavy feet shuffle forward — right back into the circle of your crooked arms.

You welcome me home the same way you used to when the top of my head barely grazed your wide hips.

Your arms hold me too tightly, your index finger will leave a bruise,

and yet — they don't hold me at all.

I feel the familiar wetness behind my eyes,

let myself weep into the wisps of your now coarse grey hair

Inside your arms, my body hears you breathe an anthem—

welcome home — you say — your chin biting sharply into my scalp.

But inside, all the parts I've always felt mattered more, all the parts your arms couldn't quite seem to hold, thrash about, flailing violently

—

Leaving bruises no one can see, sores I'm too afraid to let anyone get close to.

This is the hollow sequences of things, a fractured dance I never asked to be invited into in the first place. My body keeps you breathing, helps you rid yourself of ghosts you've never been brave enough to mention.

Fists on flesh—a self made ventilator,

The only thing putting air back into organs that have been rotting from the start.

In the end, you'll send me away into the world — clothed with new ways of feeling lonely. I'll stumble off — stay away long enough to imagine you're dead.

But it's just a trick.

Because deep down, I'm not sure I'm ready to give you up.

PART II

efore I drifted off to sleep I always found myself uttering my hopes into the blank space. At the time I wouldn't have called them prayers. You have to believe in something in order to pray, it's a rule, and at the time the only thing I believed in was how much a person could hurt you. My hopes back then were simple: all I wanted was to wake up at my own volition. Not to the sound of her footsteps moving toward the bedroom door, not to her weight making a dent in my small body, not to the sound of my sister screaming. Later in life, when all the soot had finally been scoured from my body, I'd come to savor the mornings when I would sigh awake, let my eyes adjust to the sanctuary of my tiny home. I'd speak out into the light, this time little utterances of gratitude, always beginning with "hello, home."

But I am getting ahead of myself.

On that night, I closed my eyes and whispered into the blackness. I remember wanting to weep from the volume of silent hopes. If any part of it felt the most like bondage, it was this; the parts of me that insisted on believing there could be more than being scared, slithering and roaring inside me. I pulled the pillow from underneath my head and pressed it firmly into my face, pressing and pushing and willing those hopes into smothered submission, or myself to sleep, whichever happened first.

I dreamed of what it must feel like to laugh when you are free. What it must feel like to have the stronghold of fear unclasped from around your neck, your wrists, your entire body even, limbs creaking as they stretched outward and upward, that creaking the sound of newfound freedom. I dreamed of my daddy walking in the front door of that old townhouse, arms extended outward inviting me into the embrace I'd been waiting shamelessly for. I pressed my face into his white shirt, dug my fingers into his back; he still smelled the same. Even in my dreams I was weighed down with unspeakable hopes. This time they shouted, "let this be real, let this be real." And it was real. It was real until, on that day, my dreaming was pierced by familiar sounds, howls that reached inside greedily, ripping me from his arms. I think I collected some of his skin under my fingernails as souvenirs. It happened so suddenly, I didn't have time to grieve the loss of his arms around me.

By this time my ears were highly attuned to the sound an object makes when it connects with flesh. The sound the heel of a shoe makes, at first a whistle when flying backward, as if in warning, and then a sharp crack as it causes ripples against tender skin. These are not the sounds a person should have to become accustomed to, but I have learned that you don't choose all the lessons that you will eventually learn in this life.

My feet were moving before my eyes had fully opened, carrying me across the hall. I saw Her hovering there (I was right about the shoe, possibly I could have guessed the exact one from the other room, but this is not a particular skillset I wish to boast about) above my sister, now crouched on the floor. Her body was pressed into the carpet, arms up, eyes wide with fear. When I remember that moment my sister always seems so small. In fact in all my remembering, we always seem so small. It's puzzling because by that time, we were probably the same size as Her in stature. But terror, it is a powerful thing. It can trick you right out of believing that you are strong and big. It can steal your agency and your voice. It just paralyzes your awareness of yourself because there isn't room for you. There is only Her, and you just have to give all your energy to watching and waiting and staying one step ahead.

"Stop," I must have screamed, rushing over. I knew as I wrapped my hands around her thick arm what I was inviting, but by now my sister and I had mastered the ability to share the burden of pain. I don't remember the next part. Or perhaps I do, but I don't want to. I don't want to remember what she did next, I don't want to remember which parts of me hurt next, don't want to reacquaint myself with the sound of sole or fist or plastic against flesh. I don't want to remember the frenzy of limbs flying, the shouts, the accusations, the threats. I don't want to remember my sister's naked body, my mother shoving underwear down her throat to silence her. I don't want to remember that this was all over a missing jacket. I don't want to remember. Don't make me remember the sound a voice makes when it is pleading in fear for it to stop, the ache of the heart to simply be believed for once.

AND THEN A CAR horn bellowing from our driveway. You will laugh when I tell you that even now I can remember the tone it made, clear and distinct, puncturing the chaos for just a moment. Her hand was still raised in the air but this time no sharp crack to follow. She ran back to her bedroom and fetched her things, late for work, her ride waiting. She pushed her head into the doorway one more time, hands haphazardly smoothing her wig back into it's place,

"If you don't find it before I get home, I will finish what I started. I will beat you through the night," she said.

It turns out you don't need objects to cause someone's skin to shudder. Sometimes you just need words.

I have gone over this in my mind a million times, played it back, slowed it down, torn it to shreds. Sometimes I think maybe we could have stayed, maybe we could have survived the night. Maybe. But with our backs pressed into the edge of that bed, my baby sister cradled in my arms, I looked up at my big sister's face. I saw that her song of optimism had died. Her face frightened me, skin under eyes inflated. I wondered what she saw when she looked at me. I closed my eyes and listened for the roar of hopes, but there was nothing. There was nothing.

I had wanted to die so many times. I'd imagined all the ways I could do it without making a sound. I had wished I was strong enough to complete the task, fantasized about what stillness would feel like, how one quick slice could finally bring the peace I was famished for. My sister had gotten closer than me, swallowed pills, but not enough. Mum only chuckled when she discovered the empty bottle on the bathroom floor. Apparently not even the potential of death could soften her. But on that day, some stubborn streak slithered its way up from some unseen place inside me and I thought to myself, if I die it will be because I choose to die, not because she kills me. I didn't want this to be the way my life ended, crouched on the grey carpet in terror. The words I said next changed everything. I still wear those words as a cape of responsibility around my shoulders, those words, and worse, their consequences, constantly pulling me backwards into places I never intended for us to go. They turned us into orphans. They changed my sisters. They changed me. They left my mother barren, the fruit of her womb snatched out from under her. Sometimes I don't know if it was selfish.

Is it selfish to want to live?

"We can't stay here," I finally whispered, "she will kill us."

Possibly you are now shaking your head as you read this, unconvinced that life can hinge so desperately on the location of an article of clothing. I understand. It seems so insignificant, like nonsense, a jacket. Years later, she told my sister that she'd found the jacket on the back of her chair at the office. I don't know why she told her. Maybe it was the only version of an apology she could muster. Or maybe her insides required her to confess. I wish I could have watched that day unfold on split screens. Screen A: three girls fly about the house, opening drawers, craning their necks into corners and under beds, searching one more time just in case the jacket ended up in the wrong place at the last visit to the laundromat. Screen B: Mum walks into work, eyes land almost immediately on brown jacket hanging lazily on the back side of her chair. I wonder what mothers think about after they have left their children bleeding on the floor. Do they watch their fingers moving over their keyboards and feel disgusted that these very same hands could cause such damage? Do they spend the day swallowing back tears, their bodies awash with tremors of remorse? Do they? Do you think the sight of that jacket ignited the spark that would finally send blood pumping back to her heart?

If it did, she never let on.

Brows wet, we perched once more on the edge of the bed. Our hands were empty.

"We have to go," one of our voices sliced through the fog.

I descended the stairs to the main floor, picked up the phone and dialed the phone number of my german teacher. I spewed the whole story out in between gasps, my heart threatening to fly right out of my chest. She had heard these stories before. Had heard about the reports made about the closed door happenings of that townhouse. Children's services had come. They'd come and they'd left and more scars were added as a penalty.

"Please. Help us."

People will think leaving was an easy choice. I've been called brave for picking up the phone and calling for help. But sometimes people don't want to hear that bravery comes at a cost. Sometimes you are only brave because you have run out of options. Sometimes you are only brave because the part of you that has been waiting to be held has finally given up and now all that is left is survival. Sitting in that taxi, our shoulders pressed against each other, plastic bag of clothes limply in my lap, fist full of cash, I turned my head to look back. I let the tears I had been holding in drip down my face. We were escaping because we wanted to live, but we were also leaving our mother. Please don't miss this part, I beg. As I write this, almost two decades later, I feel my heart constricting, the tears beginning to spill over. Even after all those years, I believed mum was in there somewhere. I wanted to stay just in case today might be the day I'd finally meet her. But, I confess, I wanted to stay alive even more. That is why I let myself take the cash from my school teacher and why I let her call a taxi to pick us up. It's why I didn't let myself think overlong about the consequences of what we were doing, how it might unloose one shackle only to tighten the grip of another.

The drive seemed to stretch on unnecessarily. I kept squeezing my sisters' hands to keep them from wailing. I couldn't deal with the sound of their own grief while trying to stay coherent. I was practicing what I had to make sure to tell whoever would be collecting our story. I could not be overly emotional in this case. The police had visited our house before. They'd seen my head sliced open. I was sure they could hear my bloody shirt crying out from the next room. They'd asked and I had fabricated some disorganized story about walking into a door foolishly, my eyes attempting to convey the truth without having to utter the words. I could feel her eyes examining me, scorching me in silent warning. The police left. So you understand why, on that car ride to the hospital, I forced my emotions back and made sure this time they would intervene. I had learned that police were not moved by emotion. They were not moved by blood. They were moved by logic. By facts.

I stuffed the cash in the taxi driver's hand. Then a whirlwind of arms and voices as we were ushered to separate rooms. I felt trapped in the blankness. Can someone explain to me the reason that hospital rooms are tinted in the most unnatural shade of white? Do you know? It is not for the benefit of the patient, I will tell you. You can hear your own heartbeat bouncing off corners that suddenly feel like they are pressing up against you. I focused on the doorknob, waiting and willing it to turn, until finally, one loud knock and a twist.

First a police officer, hatless, bald, asking me what happened. I told him the truth, but just the facts. I didn't cry, I didn't let my voice crack. I told him, "If you will not help us, then just take us home quietly before she returns from work. Because if she finds out we tried to escape, and then you take us home, she will kill us."

Now a social worker, kinky black hair, mustard dress, asking me the same questions. I told her wearily, "If you will not help us, then just take us home quietly before she returns from work. Because if she finds out we tried to escape she will kill us."

Now a man with a camera. He asked a different question, something about bruises and scars. He wanted his camera to capture the evidence of abuse. For this part, I could not keep my eyes from being a little bit wet. I steadied myself by breathing deeply and I showed him what was still visible. I wanted him to leave. I wanted to scream. I wanted to laugh. I wanted to hide underneath the paper covering the hospital table. I wanted to ask him to lay me down and cut me open in a straight line so he could get a full picture of the scars he was asking about. Not all forms of abuse are not visible to the human eye. They cannot be developed in a dark room and printed on paper, you understand? And in any case, I am a black girl, in case you have forgotten by now. Bruises? You know, *black* and blue? Even those are camouflaged by nature. I wanted to throw his flashing camera against the nearly white walls. It was as if my pain was invisible, as if he was trying to distill thirteen years of abuse into a few pictures. But he was missing it. He was missing me. I let him finish and then I told him, "If you will not help us, then just take us home quietly before she returns from work. Because," and this time my voice did splinter slightly, "she will kill us."

SKIN

The darkness of my skin forgave your madness
    Sooner than my heart did
    The sound of your hands on my smallness
    The snap of your wrist
    The whip of that now aged leather belt
    The crack in the plastic of that hanger
    Finally breaking against my body
    That crack - a welcome chorus of mercy

I wept silently in my twin sized bed
    Touched the tender places
    I prayed for the scars to be visible just once
    So that someone could see what your hands did to me
    But my skin was against me
    And by morning—
    On the outside of me
    Nothing

In the silence of the hospital room, my sisters locked behind their own doors, the fullness of what we had done came for me, one more visitor with its list of questions. The clanging of potential outcomes shook the tears loose from behind the wall I had told them to wait behind. The thought of her finding out we had attempted to leave was causing my insides to tremble so violently, I had to close my eyes to settle the nausea. It was not the idea of death that frightened me the most, you see. It was the way my mind was twisting together stories of what I would have to first endure before my heart finally flatlined.

Now a knock on the door, social worker, kinky black hair, mustard dress. She touched my shoulder in comfort but it caused me to flinch. I was tired. Tired of being touched and questioned, tired of waiting. The clock was ambling toward four o'clock, knocking off time, and I wanted someone to tell me what I should be feeling so I didn't have to try to figure it out on my own. I had used all my energy to convey the desperation I felt, so I turned away and waited in silence.

"We are going to place you in a foster home for the night," she said.

I am sure she said other things but they mattered very little to me at the time. She led me to a room where my sisters were already waiting. I stepped inside and waited for her to shut the door before we all collapsed into each other in a frenzy of tears and whispers. I pulled big sister's body against my own. I breathed some of her magic into me, breathed out some of my vigilance into her. Maybe it wasn't fair to put that inside of her, to contaminate her with the fear and watchfulness, but I had the feeling that we would need these pieces of each other to carry us through. We let our arms draw a circle around baby sister, squeezed and squeezed and squeezed while our tears dropped into her black hair. I wish we had hugged each other harder and longer. I wish we had laughed instead of cried. I wish we had known that this would be the last time that we would be together in this way for a long time, in some ways forever. But they forgot to tell us.

. . .

IT WAS dark when I loaded my body into the back of another car. As I slumped into the seat I had the feeling that I had lived an entire lifetime in one day. I didn't know yet if it was a lifetime I should be proud of. My legs were shaking while the tears kept dripping down my face. I gripped the handle of the car door as if to keep myself from slipping into something dark and dangerous. I was slippery and on the edge, I could feel it calling out to me. I let my other hand rest on my thigh, let it pat my leg gently as if to say, shhhh - it is going to be okay. It was a lie I had recycled over and over again to keep myself going. My feelings would not untangle themselves into anything decipherable and so how could I know if this car was taking me into freedom or further into despair? I kept my eyes looking out the window. I let them trace the shapes of houses and streets I had never encountered before. And when the eyes tried to drift into the car, to not only look but to see, I shook my head and told them, "No!" I could not let the eyes see the empty space of seat beside me. Could not bear to meet the reality of this sister separation. I had to keep looking outside because I was afraid if I let the eyes look elsewhere, the grief would rise up and strangle the remaining life right out of me. And there was hardly any life left as it was.

Before being ushered into the car, they finally told us where we would be spending the night: big sister in a psychiatric ward on suicide watch, baby sister at a children's home, and me at a foster home. I was seeing social worker's mouth making shapes while she was saying the words. I was hearing the words as they floated out of her and across to me, seemingly devoid of any real emotion. Her words were slotting together to build a world I never knew existed, like some kind of twisted poetry. I wanted to scream. I wanted to weep. I wanted to rewind the day and start again. I wanted to know what they had told my mother. Policeman said they had tried to go to the townhouse but no one was home. He said they left a post-it note on the door. I wondered if this was standard procedure, to rip three children from a mother's care with some words scribbled carelessly on a square piece of neon paper. And why did I feel sorry for her? I breathed in the empty space of the car's backseat, closed my eyes and imagined the split screen reality of the day. Screen A: Middle sister in humid sedan, social worker whispering reassurances that are flying out the open window. Screen B: mother comes home to post it note in the middle of the peeling wooden door. She rushes inside and goes from room to room but there is nothing. There is no one. I wonder what mothers think about after they suddenly find themselves childless. Do they fall to the ground in agony? Do they sigh in relief? Do they rewind the day and tremble at the blood on their hands? Do they?

If they do, she never let on.

LEMONWOOD TRAIL

I measure my life by Lemonwood Trail;
    the seasons saunter by - changing air
    against my aging membranes and yet
    there is only before and after
    that crumbling excuse for a home
    lonesome on the corner.
    I never cry in the day but baby—
    when the sun sets, I hold my labored breath
    and she comes for me
    scrapes her decaying teeth against my larynx and
    demands to breathe.
    She lets me have my false peace in the day
    but when the night comes
    she shakes her chalky bones
    rattling her malnourished flesh
    inside my eardrums
    and baby—
    the mother in me?
    she comes for me.
    I measure my life by Lemonwood Trail;
    gin and tonic in one hand
    soggy cigarette clasping onto
    the loose skin of my chapped lips
    I slip into the bathtub in my frayed neglige
    one hand pressed against my eyes
    but baby—
    this is a useless barrier
    she has come with her rolodex
    screaming 'penance' with such force
    all my armor sinks
    holds me down
    forces my eyelids open
    slips her skinny arms

into the cavity of my chest
sets my dislocated heart in it's place
a backwards exsanguination
that renders me utterly human
and baby—
the mother in me?
she comes for me
I measure my life by Lemonwood Trail;
images floating up to the surface
of this crude darkroom
every act of torture fully on display
a consentless reacquainting
with the reality of me
but baby—
the blood will not stop rushing inward
until I am chewing at my wrists
screaming for relief
pulse echoing in every corner
of this one man torture chamber
sobs slithering upward
your spilled blood
shared blood
whistling through the air
until I am face to face with your eyes
saturated in fear
and baby—
the mother in me?
she comes for me
I measure my life by Lemonwood Trail
everything before that note
on the chaffing wood door
and everything after
and baby—
the mother in me?
she comes for me

W hen we got to the house, foster mother met us at the door. She had her silk bonnet set against her hair and an oversized t-shirt hanging around her heavy frame. As social worker walked away I wondered how delivering a child into someone's care could feel so transactional, but I didn't bother asking. I let foster mother guide me wordlessly and through the dimly lit house, down a hallway and into a room with an empty bunkbed for me to sleep in. I could hear the sleep sounds of other children filling up the room. I had no clothes to change into. No toothbrush to push against my teeth. So I urinated in the unfamiliar bathroom as the only familiar pre-bedtime ritual. As I looked into the mirror while washing my hands, I no longer recognized the face looking back at me. It didn't frighten me. I knew the eyes were still doing what I had ordered them to do. Look but do not see. Do not see.

Laying on my back in the bottom bunk, I couldn't seem to stop the shivers traveling through my body. I stared up at the mattress holding another girl suspended above me and I wondered what my sisters were doing. The loneliness felt unbearable, thick like plastic wrapped around my face. This is the point in the story where people begin to think of us as resilient and brave. But I will tell you the truth, this is the point in the story where I fall asleep wondering if I have made the biggest mistake of my life.

That night I dreamed I was a sheep contained inside the belly of a wolf. I dreamed I used my hooves to press against the belly until I burst through. I climbed out and smelled the blood and guts saturating the wool of my coat; the cost of liberation. I dreamed I roamed dizzily into a cool stream to wash myself. I dreamed the smell released itself from me but I remained stained with pink. I dreamed that though the wolf was gone, the wolf was still with me.

I MUST CONFESS these next days are hard for me to write about. I was there, of course, living through the blur of court dates and questions. I was there crying into the phone with german teacher's voice on the other end. I was there begging social worker to find a way to contact

159

my father. I was telling her he would come, if he knew, he would come. I was there living but I wasn't alive, do you understand me? I have worked hard for many years to reconnect all the emotional wires that had to remain unplugged and have done so with relative success. But these first days of my new life and world - I cannot seem to retrieve the emotional data. Sometimes I get close but the fear still holds me at bay from reconnecting. If I feel it all - I'm afraid it could kill me. But for you, I will do my best.

I startled awake on the sharp intake of breath. Evidently the shaking had not ceased in the night. I let my eyes wander around the bedroom, took in the other set of bunk beds against the opposing wall and the blind shuttered window in the middle. I noticed the clothes piled against the floor and the tiny television perching atop a tall chest of drawers. I could see the bodies of other children making lumps in each of the beds and I wondered about them. What lifetimes had they lived in the space of a day that had brought them to this place? I wondered if they too had cables of fear running through their bodies, tying their bellies in knots. Laying there with the sun starting to paint the bedroom in stripes, all I wanted to do was fall asleep and never wake up again. All I wanted was an open field in which I could lay down and rest my tired spirit. I rolled over on my back and closed my eyes. I felt like my insides were alive with every possible feeling, but I couldn't grab onto a single one. I kept conjuring up images of my sisters, one being monitored constantly so that she didn't spill her own blood and end up a frozen body on the floor somewhere, and the other, just a baby, weeping into her pillow in a shelter with other kids piled on either side of her. I felt responsible, like I had somehow failed them. I wanted to release the scream that was expanding inside my chest. I wanted to run.

The house started to come awake. I could hear the bodies in the bunk beds squirming, a mug being set loudly on the counter in another room. I kept myself still and my eyes squeezed shut. The tears were building behind them again. I breathed and counted. Did it again. I knew that once I opened up my eyes what was real would only become more so. Now a toilet flushing and foster mother's voice.

Heavy feet on the ceramic floor. Breathing and counting and trying to gently coax the eyes to open. A bed creaking, the push of a button. The loud and sexual moaning of a woman filling up the room. The eyes flew open and there on the tiny television, naked bodies writhing around. The mouth fell open and the tears spilled over as I glanced around the room. I saw the other girls sitting upright in their beds watching me. I felt like an animal under observation. I sat there shaking while they pointed at me and the girl with the long brown hair and big round eyes laughed at my response.

Let me tell you about dissociation please. At first I am there in the bed. I feel my mouth hanging open and I feel the tears wetting my cheeks. I am there and my insides are a cacophony of different feelings. I am part fear, part shock, part intrigue and part, shamefully, arousal. And then I am lost to myself. I am lost to myself and to the room around me. I am away but I cannot tell you where because the other place is nameless, do you understand me? I am away until I am no longer away. Until a loud bang on the bedroom door deposits me back inside my body and I am suddenly blinking to reorient myself so I can begin catching up on what I have missed while I have been drifting— while I have been gone.

The room was empty but the house was very much alive. Everything seemed to be moving quickly and on maximum volume but I was frozen and I didn't know what I should do. I didn't know where my place was inside this world. I stayed in the bed with my knees pulled close to my chest. I was angry at the way I was coming undone. "You need to get it together" I kept saying to myself, over and over and over again. Like a chant set against my racing heartbeat, which was acting like the drums. The weight of all of it was crashing down against me like a bouquet of cement cinderblocks. I let my eyelids drop closed. I breathed in some air. Pressing my nails into my palms, I willed the tears back.

Here the cursor is flashing in and out and the blank space is staring at me. It is telling me to continue.

I am sitting with my back against the chair and I am just breathing. My palms are resting on my cheeks in an effort to hold myself. I am feeling the place in my shoulder that burns when I am on the edge of fragmentation. When I come in contact with pain and want to numb. And that's when I whisper to myself "you can feel this and breathe. you can breathe." A new anthem. Because for so long I didn't know I could keep breathing. It wasn't allowed. If I tell this story I have to stay connected. I have to keep holding hands with that little baby in the bunk bed all those years ago. I have to do that so she can tell the part of this story that is hers. So that we can continue to integrate all the pieces. So that as I write I am able to look at her and nod my head - so she isn't alone any more. It's hard to write this. It's still so hard to let these words wriggle out of me. To organize those days that felt so frenetic. So hopelessly alone. I want to rip the pages to shreds because I don't want to remember. Even now - I don't want to remember. The scream that was vibrating inside my body and expanding my chest then - it's still here. Jesus, I still want to run.

A MINUTE, please.

WHAT DO I DO?

What am I supposed to do here? When I feel myself caught in a
rollercoaster
    First upward toward the apex of this pain and rage
    and then falling into what feels like
    impending death. When,
    as I claw to string myself back together
    stitch by bloody stitch and bone by bone
    in hopes of restoring the wholeness that should have never been
    severed and dislocated to begin with...
    I can feel the edges of death calling out to me
    like the clear blue expanse of the sea
    or even an open field
    An invitation into stillness that shutters the eyes of an aching heart
    Puts it to sleep and
    calls it into a nothingness that could be
    sheer bliss or something like it
    It is here, I admit
    when the pain meets the longing in an age old and
    bitter embrace
    that the soul departs and returns to rattling against the rigid bars
    of long ago constructed
    cages
    Here when the pain splits the silence with a resounding - "why"
    and a whimper
    that the edges threaten to fall away
    where I begin to feel myself slipping away
    receding to somewhere beyond here
    reaching for the nameless place
    beyond pain and beyond breath
    to become no one in the nameless place
    to become nothing in the nameless place
    to become void inside the void
    What do I do?

The splintering away has both kept me alive
and cost me my life so—
do I fall away and welcome the familiar lullaby of
dissociation
let it sing me to sleep and
divorce the soul from the body in order to stay alive or
do I stay and by staying
feel and by feeling
resuscitate the sleeping self
shake her from her slumber
invite her into something more than staying alive
invite her into living?
And if living means feeling
yet the body perceives feeling as dying then—
What do I do here?

F inally the foster mother ambled into the room, sharing her body weight with a wooden cane. I sat upright and watched her. She stopped in front of me and gave a smile that never reached the center of her round eyes, and used her index finger to beckon me out of the bottom bunk. I followed her out of the room. I don't mean to sound dramatic, but I had the feeling like I was walking around completely naked in front of a house of strangers. Have you ever felt the same? As if all your inside bits are just hanging out exposed on the outside of your body and there is nothing you can do to cover them up. If you have ever felt like that, that is the feeling you can insert here. Foster mother told me to sit at the kitchen table and wait. The other children were moving around the house in a rush. I go away again. I come back. They are sitting in front of me, three girls, eating dry cereal out of bowls. No one speaks and I comfort myself with the familiarity of this kind of tense silence. The kind of silence that is dripping with warning. This is one of those houses where noise is a nuisance and there are consequences for being a nuisance. I take note.

One more girl walked out of a separate room further down the hallway. She had the type of gait that announced that she is in charge in some way. She was the one who introduced the other girls, and herself as well. Foster mother was her biological mother, she said, and suddenly the authority in her gait made sense. She existed in between worlds, I realized. It was clear when foster mother entered the room that the same rules applied to her. I saw the way she stood with her back rigid as her mother moved through the kitchen, refilling her coffee cup and leaving brown drips on the counter. She was the same as the rest of us, but also different. A daughter and not just a temporary acquisition.

The next days passed with a flurry of court dates and social workers and mostly, a blur saturated in fear about the impending moment when I may have to see Mum again. The other children would go off to school and I was left in the empty house with foster mother, doing everything I could to stay out of the way. It wasn't difficult. I was already accustomed to making myself as small as possible. Social worker would come to the house to check in, to ask more questions. Every time I would interrogate her about what she was doing to get ahold of my daddy. It was the footage and flashbacks of the second soul that was inside him that kept me asking, no— pleading, for her to find a way to reach him. The second soul, with the wide smile and the bare feet and the gentleness, he would come if he knew, I told her, but she never seemed to make any progress. In the evening, the phone would ring and my breath would catch as I waited and hoped the call was for me. When it was it was big sister or baby sister and a few times it was German Teacher on the other side. If it was one of my sisters on the other end, I did my best not to cry. I don't remember what we said to each other. What could we say? Everything and nothing was happening at the same time, and who has words for that sort of thing? Not me, I'll tell you the truth. When it was German teacher's voice whispering "hello" on the other end, I would weep wordlessly while she told me it would all be okay. I wanted to believe her but it was difficult. I didn't even know what "okay" meant anymore. The only thing I knew for certain was the moment I was living in. Beyond that, I couldn't say, I couldn't see and I certainly couldn't believe in anything, especially "okay."

I was thankful for the days when social worker picked me up to take me to the court house. Even though those days were the most ridden with anxiety, every court date also meant an opportunity to see my sisters. The three of us piled into waiting rooms with other children, now called wards of the state. We clutched each other's hands, the beginnings of our separateness already starting to take shape. I felt like I was losing more of them and more of myself every time we parted ways, unsure of when we would see each other next.

At one of these court dates, the judge asked us if we had anything we wanted to say to Mum. I was uncharacteristically brave, or maybe I was desperate, I can't be sure. I nodded at social worker to take me into the room. My heart was doing something unusual as I followed behind her, as if it were trying to excavate a trench through my chest and escape. Like it wanted to stay behind in the waiting room while I behaved recklessly. I stepped inside the stuffy room. The terror was making my stomach upset but I kept walking forward until seated in front of the courtroom. I wished I had prepared what I wanted to say, written it down on red lined index cards, distilled all the pain from the last thirteen years into something clear and distinct that I could offer her, finally granted the opportunity to speak. But I didn't prepare, and perhaps, you never can prepare for the moment when you look your mother in the eye and beg her to tell you why she could not ever find the will to offer any tenderness to you. I kept my head tilted down toward the floor, while the judge invited me to begin. I had the feeling everyone was waiting for me to talk about the things that she had done, those weighty stories of abuse, of neglect, of terror. But for me there was only one question that really mattered in the end. And so with tears crowding themselves in my eyes, I took a deep breath and looked up into the eyes of this woman who felt part mother and part monster. It was the mother in her I was addressing.

"Why can't you love me?" I whispered.

MOTHER

Mother, you're the orphan now.
    Shut up in your three bedroom apartment— alone.
    Abandoned permanently by the offspring of your womb.
    I shamefully think you deserve this.
    You did this to us, to our family-- to me.
    You marred the love that should have bound us together.
    You marred me,
    Mother.
    I hate you. For all the tears. And all the bothersome layers
    Of hurt and filth that coat the insides of me.
    I hate you--
    Because there is no hurt big enough
    No hole deep enough inside of me
    To swallow up and bury deep
    The love my heart feels,
    Traitorously,
    For you.
    Mother.
    I hate me.
    I hate the softness of me-
    For feeling pity or something kin to it
    I hate that I long for you to know the love
    That you so viciously denied me.
    Mother. Mother.
    Mama.
    It does not seem fair that I should sit here contemplating how
    To share a greater love with you
    You don't deserve it--
    But I am better than you, aren't I?
    Am I?

Her eyes did not even flicker, her body did not flinch as her heart registered the trembling voice of her baby. I wanted to sprint out of my chair, open her mouth wide and get a glimpse of what was happening inside of her. I wanted to crawl in, slither down her throat and use my hands to rub against her insides until they warmed. I wanted her to say something. I just wanted something that I could squeeze my hands around, anything to make sense of her maternal detachment. We studied each other in silence until she turned her face away from me. That was when I felt the hope sail out of me, that naive wish that there existed some chord of love between mother and child that could revive whatever piece of her had been sleeping for so long. Her silence was one last landmine eviscerating my insides, sending the shattered pieces of my heart flying around bloodily inside my chest cavity. I looked at the top of her neatly styled wig and heard the flatline of love echoing through the room. And then I was a lost to myself again, drifting weightlessly in the place without a name.

WHISPER

We said farewell with a whisper
    My heart ardently appealing to your heart
    Pleading
    As I chronicled before watching eyes
    All the ways your hands had marred me.
    How your delicate fingers
    Had twisted in my flesh
    The way your manicured nails punctured
    My face
    Wood splintered across my back
    My shaking hands pulling glass from the nest of
    My hair
    Swollen
    My blood dripping on the floor

A mess I'd soon pay for.

"Why can't you love me?" my whisper ricocheted off the concrete walls-
    You replied only with a gaze
    Of hardened indifference.
    And your eyes reflected the truth
    That I was nothing to you
    But a troublesome mistake
    That your love outgrew

We said goodbye on that whisper
    You exhaled and freed yourself of me
    I held my breath
    Breathed in your hatred
    And neglect
    And swallowed you down deep inside me
    And on the outside I was strong

My walls neatly built
Unbreakable fortress
Yet on the inside
Blackness seized my sight
And I was blind
Barely breathing
Frantically swimming
Through the flood conceived
By my unshed tears.

And my soul floated in the darkness
Condemned to the shadows
Of the words your lips had sown--

I was who you said I was.
A blemish
Without worth
Alone-
Ashamed-

Alone.

That night I dreamed I was a wolf contained inside the belly of a sheep. I dreamed I used my teeth to gnaw a hole through the esophagus until I burst through. I climbed out and smelled the blood and guts of the pink wooled carcass as I kicked it aside. I dreamed that though I was sheep born to a wolf, I could be a sheep no longer.

B ack at the foster home, I moved around from room to room numb and in disbelief. The foster mother was disengaged until one of the children gave her a reason to engage. Then she would expand as if someone was pumping air into her body and fill the house with her rumbling voice. She'd at times use her cane against a shin or backside. I made myself small and emerged only to use the bathroom, eat a handful of dry cereal or to answer the phone. I only remember eating cereal while I was there, often not even bothering with a bowl and spoon. I'd stuff my pudgy hand directly into the box and eat a few handfuls before ambling back to bed. When foster mother had shut herself away in her corner of the house, the other girls would laugh and dance and for a time I couldn't be bothered to join them. As lonely as I felt, I also felt terrified to begin living as if this was now my home. I couldn't accept it. Engaging felt like giving in to this new world, and I closed my fists in resistance as long as I could. Every day the doubts about what we had done were eating at me like maggots. At least with Mum I had the companionship of my sisters. But here, in this tiny brick house, I felt completely alone. The other girls frightened me, my age but with knowledge of life that I couldn't relate to. They climbed into bed with each other at night, often inviting me to participate, porn glistening off the television screen. I wanted to know why people were always offering to explore my body in the night. I felt trapped, embarrassed and, mostly, ashamed at the way my body felt as my eyes drifted up toward the television screen.

About a week into my stay, I was enrolled in a school close to the home, handed two changes of clothes and expected to make it work. It wasn't difficult. Vanity was not a high priority of mine at the time. At school I sat in the unfamiliar classrooms with my head on the table. I didn't talk to anyone and I didn't complete a single assignment. At lunch girls would make attempts to speak to me, but I couldn't seem to muster up the energy to engage. I'd carry my lunch tray to the end of the emptiest table and sit alone. As you now know, this was very unlike me. School had always been the place I thrived, the place I came alive. But as I have said, at this time "me" had disappeared and all that was left was my body floating through the days like an apparition, dressed in an unseemly blue velour tracksuit. Every day felt the same. For a long time, I under reported the amount of time I was in that house. It wasn't intentional. It's just - I couldn't really say with certainty. If someone had said it had been a day I would have believed them. If someone had said it had been a lifetime it would have also felt true.

Eventually resistance gave way to acceptance. As one week rolled into two and then more. As the hope continued to leak out of me, resistance gave way to acceptance, and I began to engage. I danced in the bathroom with the other girls, learning to grind my hips from side to side as Sean Paul poured out of the radio speakers. I let them push an earring through the cartilage of my right ear. My body jumped as I heard the slight pop as the small fake diamond earring cleared the tissue and made it to the other side. I let them glue long wavy weave tracks into my hair with thick black hair glue. I felt like a mannequin being dressed and molded to fit into my new reality. Late at night the daughter's cell phone would ring and on the other end would be one of the men she said lived in the neighboring apartment complex. One night he had a friend with him. She put me on the phone, telling him I had big full lips. I put the phone to my ear and his voice wriggled in, raspy and deep. He asked me about my lips but I had nothing to say. I had not ever given my lips much thought, honestly. He wanted to know what I could do with those full lips and I felt my stomach turn over in terror. I handed the phone back to the daughter and after a few seconds of silence, her laughter filled up the space.

"He's afraid you might be boring," she said. I said nothing back.

That night I laid in bed pondering what it meant to be boring. I felt confused. I couldn't understand why I felt so rejected. I wished for my big sister, who always seemed to understand men better than I did. I wanted to be desirable too.

A few nights later, the foster daughter told her mother we were going for a walk. Before we went, I stood still while they dressed me.

While they painted black eyeliner on my eyelids and smeared cherry lip gloss over my apparently full lips. They tugged my shirt down further to expose the smooth domes of my developing breasts. They curled my new weave into bouncy waves. I looked up into the mirror and someone was there looking back at me. Her eyes were scared but I thought she looked pretty. It was, in part, a powerful feeling, to see myself turned into something unrecognizable. When they were satisfied we left the apartment and walked down the street in a line. I knew the truth about this walk we were on, that we were going to meet the men whose voices filled our ears every night. I felt the same as that long ago night in K-town when I had been allowed out with the older girls: equal portions of fear and excitement. I wanted to get this right. All I wanted was to fit in somewhere. All I wanted was to be desirable for once in my life.

When we got upstairs, one of the men poured me a drink and slid me into place across his lap. I didn't quite know what to do with myself so I sat perfectly still and as straight as possible. I could hear the blood rushing inside my ears. He started whispering to me while his hand rubbed my leg. Whispering to me while his hand moved higher and squeezed itself in between my thighs, "to keep warm," as he said before it settled itself against me for a while. My body was trembling and my eyes were becoming congested with tears. I focused on the room, on the way the lights were dim. I focused on the other girls laughing. I focused hard so that I wouldn't feel his hands on my skin, the way they felt rough on my belly and then on my breast. I focused so I didn't feel his tongue using my neck like a slide. So I didn't feel his larger hand guiding my small hand to feel his hot, hard skin while he moaned into my ear and taught my hand how to move against him in a steady rhythm while he groaned throatily in unison with his shuddering body. The tears spilled over.

I WANTED to be grown up and brave. But my body wouldn't let me.

. . .

I WAS THERE and my body was with me
   with me but not mine
   with me but yours

I CRIED.
   No, I wailed.

I GO AWAY. My soul ejected itself from my body and I was watching from above while the body was thrashing around on the wooden floor. I come back. The girls gathered me together. They helped me stand up. The men said that I had to go. I walked the distance home alone and in the dark with my chin tucked to my chest. I walked home in a blur of confusion and shame, tripping over my own feet as I fought back the tears.

It occurs to me that here you may be thinking that I should have been grateful that the night ended as it did. You are thinking that I should have been grateful that my reaction caused those men to lose interest and send me home on my own before they had, perhaps, done more than use my hands to make themselves moan while they stroked my bare skin. I understand. Much graver things could have happened. So let us pause here for me to say - in hindsight, I am of course grateful. I really am. But I have also promised to tell you the full truth and the full truth is that in the moment gratitude was not a feeling I could hold onto. In the moment it was an internal agony that was making my shoulders slump and causing the tears to start seeping out of my eyelids like tiny rivers. I was furious. I was relieved. I was in shock. I didn't know which one to focus on first. I didn't know what to think of myself anymore, either. I admit that some part of me did want to be held; to be touched and desired. I wanted to offer myself up and I wanted someone to let me know that I was worth something. I wanted *someone* to want me, do you understand me? I am not proud of it, but it is the truth. At the same time, I could feel bile rising up my

throat at the idea that I would so shamelessly offer myself up to someone. Did I offer myself or was I offered? Should I hate my body for
getting in the way or thank it for protecting me from a further violation? At the time I couldn't be sure. I climbed into bed with the make
up still sitting on my face.

It turns out that while I was moving through my new life, drifting between states of connection and disconnection, while I was trying to absorb all the new variables that had suddenly been thrust into my hands, other parts of my life were unfolding - like another split screen. Miles and miles away German teacher was spewing pieces of the story out to her Sunday school class at church, the very same church Mum and us girls had attended together. She was, as I came to find out, crying and pleading and petitioning God, and whoever else would listen, that we needed help. She did not tell me this was happening when she called me on the phone, perhaps to protect my heart from further rupture, or just in case the plan she was piecing together did not come to fruition. In her church class there was baby sister's good friend from school, there was german teacher, and there was another couple, at the time unknown to me. That couple left church on one sunny Sunday and the husband had felt led — to clarify, here the word "led" means that something in him had felt stirred up by the story — and it had been him who had said to the wife that they should open up their home to one of us girls. For many years I had imagined it was the opposite, that it had been the wife who had said to the husband. That it had been her whose heart had been stirred and moved. Her heart had always felt so much more moveable. But I am getting ahead of myself again. The plan was unfolding like this: each one of these families would take one of us girls into their care temporarily. German teacher told me, with a slight hesitancy, that she would be taking big sister into her home and not me. I felt my heart come loose a little bit and start plummeting to the ground. She said that it was only because she thought Mum might dispute me being the one going into her care, given our closeness and Mum's jealousy over the years. I understood and it still devastated me. Baby sister would go with her friend from school and I would go with the husband and wife. Us sisters would be within three miles of one another. We would get to be close to each other, we would get to return to our schools and to our church. We would once again be able to inhabit a world that was familiar, though the circumstances of that world were now completely changed. It was a good plan, remarkable even. When it finally reached my ears my mouth dropped open. I couldn't believe it. It was as if her words were allowing the particles of the fog I had been living in to crystallize into something tangible.I felt like my chest was expanding with air as if for the first time in weeks. Maybe, I thought to myself tentatively, it really would be okay.

I spent the last of my days at that first foster home continuing to rotate between my two outfits, boycotting schoolwork, and dancing in the bathroom with my temporary sisters. Since that phone call with German teacher, something inside my body had unclenched and I was letting myself breathe a little more freely. I was letting myself soak up the rest of this transitional space, knowing it was just that, a transition. Once the plan had become more concrete, social worker drove me to my old middle school and re-registered me for class there. I walked through the hallways with tears rolling down my face. I saw the familiar faces of students I had sat across from at lunch or beside in crowded classrooms, and I wept at the recognition. It felt like they were all watching me as I went from classroom to classroom to retrieve my textbooks. Their eyes were full of questions and rumors and all the things in between but I didn't care. I didn't care at all. My eyes were saying back, I'm coming home. And wasn't school the place that felt the most like home anyway?

The morning I was to meet the couple taking me into their home, I woke up to the rumbling house one last time. I woke up to the now familiar sound of the foster mother's bare feet on the kitchen floor, her cane banging along beside her. I sat up in the bunk bed and looked around, watching one more time while the rising sun was painting the bedroom in stripes. I hoped never to return to this place or any place like it. My heart was banging around in my chest. I whispered to it gently out of fear it would become concussed. I found myself sitting on the familiar precipice of unknown. Once again I was alive with so many different emotions and I didn't know which one to focus on. I opted to let the fear have a sliver of space and pushed everything else back. I stood up and walked to the bathroom. I let the girls braid my hair into cornrows with long braiding hair while I sat on the toilet. I dressed myself in the best I had and waited. Sitting on the brown living room couch, I waited. A knock on the door. Social worker, kinky brown hair, red blouse and a small smile. I told you, life changes always seemed to announce themselves with a twist of a doorknob. She gathered me up, gathered my small plastic bag inside her hands. I said goodbye to the foster mother and followed behind the social worker. The couple was waiting by their truck, she said. I breathed to make little more space in my body for the fear as we walked toward the truck. I told my feet to keep moving even though some part of me wanted to stay frozen. When the truck doors opened I sucked air in through my teeth and watched as the couple emerged. I don't know how to explain it but to me they felt larger than life. As if I was a tiny ant in the presence of giants. The truth is they were tall but it was something other than height that was making me feel so small. It was about power. It was about my life being handed over to another grown up, and I'm sorry but I'm sure you can understand that my faith in grown ups had withered away. I took them in. The wife was standing with a broad smile on her face. Her hair was cut in a short bob and her lipstick seemed to be bright against her milky white skin. The husband was perhaps the tallest person I had ever seen. His face had a smile on it but I was having trouble getting a read on him. I wanted to find someone to hide behind but there wasn't anyone. Social worker nudged me forward. We exchanged names. They opened the back seat of their truck and I climbed in to sit beside their four year old daughter. She had the sweetest and roundest little face but I still wanted to throw up. I wanted to throw the door open and run, but the little daughter reached out and grabbed my hand, as if she could sense the the way I was teetering on the edge. She didn't know but that small hand against my larger one was calling me to stay put and stay together. I looked into her blue eyes as her face split open into a smile.

"I've always wanted a sister," she said.

There is a version of this story that ends here. There is a version where I tie things up and the story ends here. I am sure you are getting tired of having these words crawling around under your skin. I am sure you are wondering, my god, when will this girl finish talking? I am sure you are thinking, how much more of this can I take. I understand. At this point in time I was thinking something similar. There is a version of this story that ends here. It's not the truth but it would be nice to pretend, no? To tie something neat and secure around the words you have read so far so that you can push this book closed and reach the end. There is a part of me that wants to tell it like that. In fact there is a part of me that has told the story just like that. I have left some of me out in order to make myself more manageable and perhaps, more marketable as well. I have put some of me outside and left her shivering in the cold while waiting for someone to invite her inside into something warm and spacious. To let what is true be true. There is part of me that is wondering whether you will keep letting your eyes move back and forth over these pages if I keep telling the truth, or maybe you would prefer the pretend version? But the pretend version leaves some of me out in the cold and I don't think I can do that anymore, do you understand? Do you?

ONWARD

Onward. This is the word lodged in my brain today. It has something to say but I admit I'm not certain what that is or what it wants from me. I'm only certain of the tears in my eyes each time I stop and ponder it. I'm only certain that I'm soft today. For the first time in ages — I'm soft. Toward myself. Toward the life it has been and the one I hope it will become. Today the softness has sucked all the rage from my clenched fists. And they are open. They're open.

And they are marked with the word "onward."

When the rage stills, everything is so quiet. It's a little eerie, I confess. Perhaps the rage has become comforting now. I'm so familiar with it. And this anthem of onward — it is undoing my strength. It's magnifying all that has hurt. Everything that still hurts. It's inviting the grief and the dreams into this silent onward space. It's inviting the honesty of fear, and the darkness of shame.

It's whispering into the shackles of this rage — it's saying:

Onward, onward…

This fire will not eat you up — though it scorches your flesh.

Onward — it will not eat you up, girl.

It's weeping fat thick tears into this thrashing river full of question marks and shards of stolen things, it's weeping into it and saying,

Onward

Onward, girl

This water will not snatch the life from your body, though the water fill your nose, though it stings and chokes you. Though this storm feels heavy, like it is dragging you backward into darkness —

Onward

Because even backwards is forwards for you. And onward is always winning. Even when the sins done against your body and your soul are ringing inside your already shattered ear drums and even when the sight is far too frightening.

When you fear you will not breathe again.

When the dark is so solid you could lose yourself in it — even then.

Onward.

They lived on a side street that intersected the one that German teacher's house sat on. Their little girl was rambling on as we made the drive to their house, only stopping to fill her lungs with oxygen before beginning all over again. Her excitement about having a sister was endearing and a little overwhelming. You see, that excitement was knocking some of the loss inside of me loose. All she wanted was to play with Barbie dolls in the floor of her bedroom later, she was saying. I wanted the same but with my own sisters, like we once had, laughing giddily as we pressed the boy barbie and the girl barbie's lips together while the mom and dad in Parent Trap did the same on the small television screen in our bedroom. I swallowed hard and pushed the memory back.

As we continued to drive along, my ears were picking up the words that the little daughter was saying but inside my body was inflating with something adjacent to excitement, or maybe it was excitement holding hands with fear. Or maybe even hope? Whatever was happening was an unfamiliar pairing. It was because the longer we drove, the more I began to register the familiarity of the scenery. It was because as we drove by the church that ate up the entire corner of a busy street, and by my middle school and past German teacher's house my stomach was beginning to feel at home, while also holding the awareness that home meant that Mum was nearby. I felt a shiver dancing up my spine. I looked down at the little girl's hand still clutching onto mine and I wondered if she was anchoring me or if I was anchoring her. It turns out it was a little bit of both, but I will say more about that later. As I looked at her hand and up to her eyes, blue like a summer sky untouched by a single cloud, I let my heart expand a little bit to make room for her.

We went shopping on that first day. After we stopped at their house, sitting along a street with a culdesac like aunt's house had on my first days in America, and after they walked me upstairs to the bedroom that would be mine, then the wife and I got back into her car and we went shopping so that I would have more clothes to wear. I was quiet on the drive not knowing what to say to fill the space. At times I felt I was living inside a film except someone had forgotten to give me the script. Or maybe here the script would simply say *strained silence* and if so I was playing the part perfectly. We drove to an outdoor mall and moved through the stores scouring the racks to find some things I wanted to wear. The wife was kind and had a gentleness about her that I appreciated. She really did have the broadest smile I had ever seen but it did little to soothe the discomfort taking up residence inside me. I just felt so wound up and unsettled. Grateful for the new clothes but incredibly uncomfortable. I didn't know where I should be putting this experience. I am trying even now to find the words to convey what it feels like to know that by existing you are taking something from someone. Perhaps taking up a space that isn't yours. If you have ever felt like that, if that feeling has ever made a home inside your body then you can imagine that feeling here. Dependence without familiarity is a strange experience.

That night I played Barbies with the little girl on the floor of her bedroom. I had the feeling like I was floating like an orb. As if I was watching my hands move and my mouth speak yet not altogether there. Like another split screen. Screen A: I let her wrap a feather boa around my neck and put a crown on my head. I buttoned her into a princess dress and wrapped a matching boa around her. We laughed as we knelt in front of her doll house and together built a world for her collection of Barbies to live into. Screen B: Somewhere beyond skin, beyond the movements of flesh, the soul is screaming "I don't know how much more I can take" and "I wish it could all be over" back and forth like a two line song while the body smiles to maintain the strong exterior.

The next days were an attempt at settling into this new life and world that was, curiously, nestled into the bones of a previous life. The intersection was strange, that all at once everything seemed new again and at the same time incredibly familiar. We went to the same grocery store I had walked through with Mum and my sisters, on those days when, as I walked, I was trying hard to figure out what the perfect distance was to walk both behind and beside Mum. Those old habits didn't fall away. As I walked in the grocery store with the family, I kept myself behind them and I kept quiet. I felt terrified but I couldn't put it into words, so I just tried to participate in the shared experience while keeping the rest hidden. At night I wasn't sleeping. I tried because the body was so tired but everything else was wide awake and on high alert and keeping watch. When my eyes would fall heavy and sleep would come, the pictures behind my eyelids would twist into familiar and frightening experiences I never wanted to repeat. I'd turn the lights on and weep. All I wanted was a moments peace, but my hope in its existence was starting to drain out of me. In the mornings I would startle upright as soon as I heard any sound in the house. And I'd wait, not knowing what I was supposed to do next. I waited until the little girl's eager feet carried her into my bedroom. I followed her down the stairs and into the kitchen. I sat with her at the table while we ate our breakfast. I stayed quiet because I'm sorry but what do you say? I can't explain it and I don't mean to sound ungrateful but a piece of me wanted to pack my bags and run back to the first temporary house. I wanted to run hard and fast so that at least I would not be the only child inside the home who did not belong there. The only one who was a temporary acquisition. I felt like a body being tossed from place to place yet never fully settled anywhere. If you had been looking into that kitchen, you would have observed a still body at the kitchen table. But beyond skin I was writhing and twisting and screaming. Beyond the borders I was calling out to my daddy hoping that my voice would reach beyond time and space, stun him slightly then bring him to me. Or me to him, I didn't care which.

The strangeness of this intersection between the old and new life was particularly poignant when, on one of my first Sundays there, we dressed and drove to the church I had attended with Mum. Inside that church all the lives I had lived decided to make an appearance, and I was caught in the violent clash of their meeting. On one hand I was buzzing with excitement to finally be reunited with German teacher and to see the friends I had made in youth group again. I was excited that one day, when baby sister was living with her best friend and big sister with German teacher, I would also see them at church. On the other hand there would be ques-

MARJIE MONRO

tions. On the other hand there would possibly be judgment. And also, there would be Mum.

I was standing in a group in the hallway after youth group. There were, as I suspected, questions. I didn't answer because I didn't yet know how to put any or all of what was happening into words. More than questions there had been hugs and maybe even tears and it was a relief, I'll be honest. It was a relief to just be held for a moment and then caught up on who had a crush on who or reminded that the mean girls we hated were still the mean girls that we hated. Some things had stayed the same. But as I was saying, I was standing in a group in the hallway after youth group. We were getting ready to go to the main sanctuary for the boring service that we all, historically, got through by passing notes back and forth on the tithing envelopes, unless we had to sit beside our parents that day. I was standing there and I don't know how to explain it except for that it felt like suddenly my body had been plugged into an electrical outlet and started hissing with some new awareness. I knew this feeling. I looked around, letting my eyes scan the area slowly until I found her, there on the other side of the hallway. She was not close to me but she may as well have been standing a nose length away. I blinked. I froze. I felt everything in that moment like a flash. The terror, the shame, the longing, the mountain of grief. Most of me wanted to turn and bolt as far away as possible and the other wanted to run into her arms, slide down onto my knees in front of her and hope we could all start again. It hurts my body to write this, all these years later because I still feel it. I still feel the weight of that moment inside my chest like a stone. I know the things you do not yet know. I know about how the terror of seeing her there on Sundays made my mouth stretch open to social worker one day and tell her. I told her that I was terrified every time Mum looked over at me. I understand that may sound crazy, but hopefully by now I have painted this picture well enough that we understand each other. That you understand how a look can feel like a dagger or a like a grave warning. I was afraid to go to the bathroom by myself or walk the length of the hallway unaccompanied just in case I might find myself standing face to face in front of her and defenseless.

I don't know what I was asking for when I reported the fear to social worker, but I know that she told Mum what I said and that Mum had felt forced to leave the church that had become a home for her. I know because years later big sister's voice on the other side of the telephone told me that Mum had been furious and resented me for that. I know she told this story about me to whoever would listen. I can imagine the look of contempt etched into her face as she shared the story of her daughter, as if the fear I felt was irrational. As if I was just being selfish. Evicting her had never been my intent. I had never meant to hurt her, but I can still feel the sting of her resentment wrapping itself around my heart like a boa constrictor.

RIPTIDE

No one told me how the pain would sometimes come like a riptide
    a sudden disruption to the steady and newfound flow
    to the rhythm of liberation
    sudden like bony fingers encircling bony ankles and bony wrists
    in a vice grip
    like phantom hands dragging the body down
    and into the abyss of the sea

there should be a warning, surely

I steel myself for a fight - I will not go willingly
    this violent disturbance still frightens me so
    I will not go willingly and instead
    Embrace my own violent opposition to this, my littleness
    pump the limbs with vigor while imaginary bucketsful of ocean
water
    clog the lungs and invite the body to gasp against the impression
of
    suffocation — the familiar awareness of

I can't breathe

Please don't make me go back there -
    whistles out of the salt cracked mouth
    But it is not ocean water on these lips —
    just the twin salinity of tears
    rippling down the slopes of the cheeks,
    and settling on the tongue
    on my tongue
    Every ripple a thread
    every thread a memory
    every memory— *sigh
    I'd rather be caught in a riptide than this

The intensity of these currents could drown me
faster than the sea

I can't keep doing this -
    floats a thought in the unseen space called mind
    As I remain caught in the unwelcome and
    unseen intersection of invisible and unannounced triggers
    Bound in the hands of wispy apparitions I would sooner forget
    or abandon entirely
    And yet — to abandon them I abandon myself simultaneously

It hardly seems fair

That to hold myself together — I must let this pain
    take up residence
    Coax the aching limbs to stop flailing
    Stop wrestling against these sensations that do, in fact,
    belong—?
    Lie still and let the current take me
    treat it as a guide instead of an enemy
    Soften in welcome instead of harden in opposition to
    every single part of my experience

The eyes close and build a screen on the lids
    and there the memories waft by like a film
    A film but also not a film
    because the body reminds me- I was living
    through the hazy images dancing inside my mind

I freeze the frame
    I walk inside
    Make my arms a home to hold
    the pieces that suffered alone
    Listen and see and touch and whisper,
    I am so sorry — and I really am

so, so sorry

Over and over and over until
    the currents even out into something less shaky
    until the grip on the limbs loosens
    until the breath unwinds into something less staggered
    until the thought emerges with astounding clarity:

maybe compassion is liberation
    and opposition is death

Here some parts of life began to stretch out into something more stable and predictable. Some of the old fear began to release itself from my insides and make way for the mathematics and energy of another new life. I spent my time between church, school and the new home. At school the determination that lay dormant at the first foster home resurrected itself suddenly, as if in a familiar setting I could at least begin to hope again. I'd set new academic standards for myself, push until I beat my own record and then start again with a new target in mind. Honors classes turned into AP classes and AP classes turned into finding myself in a few classes on the International Baccalaureate track. I was charismatic and a favorite of my teachers. They challenged me and pushed me and fanned the flame inside me into something that was roaring with vigor. I have come to think of the white painted concrete buildings of my high school as a type of home, my teachers a type of surrogate parent that created the type of haven that invited something in me to thrive. I was a steady moving locomotive on a shaky train track I had built in secret. The scenery around me was changing but I kept my eyes on the destination.

At school I infiltrated different social groups. I won't flatter myself and say that I was popular, but I was liked and so gratefully school was never a threatening place. At lunch I was never lonely, rotating between the basketball girls and my friends from class or from choir. I ate my lunch while laughing about nothing and nonsense and felt in those moments entirely the way a teenager ought to feel. Some of my friends knew the truth of what I had been through but for the most part it felt good to keep things separate. At school the hardest things were friend break ups and being turned down by crushes. All my friends, it seemed, were falling in love for the first time and at times my heart ached and wondered why I never was chosen in that same way. One day at lunch, I sat across from a friend of mine and her girlfriend walked behind her and pulled her fallen tank top strap back into position on her shoulder. I remember watching the motion as if stunned by this simple act of adoration and care. I wondered silently if anyone would ever touch me with such tenderness. The truth was that I was starving for affection and for softness. Up to this point touch had felt violent and forceful and most times without my consent. All I wanted was touch without a penalty. I shook my head suddenly aware that these were not appropriate thoughts to be swirling mid bite of cold cafeteria pizza. I blinked to clear my head from the stupor and laughed to rejoin the conversation.

If I wasn't at school and I wasn't at the house, I was at church or with my church friends. Church for me was primarily a social event. Don't get me wrong, at the time I did believe in God and was often moved by the Christian pop lyrics we all sang in the youth worship room like we were at a concert. The neon floor picked up and reflected the lights that were shining off the beams suspended above the stage and we all swayed with our arms raised up in praise. I often wept at the images of beauty and hope being spun together through the lyrics of the songs we were singing. I wanted to believe in the sort of love the words were describing. I really wanted to believe in sovereign protection, it's just that at times I did not know where to place God within the pain I had already experience. If he was all seeing then had he been watching? What about when I had wept while my body was being violated and I prayed through gritted teeth for someone to come and save me? Had he been an unmoved spectator then? What I am saying is that the relationship between God and myself always felt complicated and strained. At times he felt eerily similar to all the other parents in my life. At times he felt like nothing more than another being that demanded gratitude and allegiance, yet left me unprotected when I was utterly defenseless. And yet I kept finding myself crawling toward him on my knees, begging him for forgiveness for who knows what and petitioning him to get me out of danger. To get me out of the pain and darkness and if possible, out of living altogether. The help never came in those ways in particular but I kept his secrets too. I raised my hands while my eyes leaked tears as I sang the worship songs and I told the story to give him credit for saving me. I joined the youth choir and went to church camp and I never told anyone about the ways my love for him was fragmented by the strange awareness that he resembled every image of parent I had ever experienced. But besides that complication I did love church. I loved meeting my friends there on Wednesday nights and catching up on our separate lives from our separate worlds. Some of my friends went to private school and another was home schooled. Another friend went to the same school as I did but our paths rarely crossed while there. We'd share the gossip and the drama and laugh about the days when some of us hated each other and the irony of now being best friends. It had happened at church camp when the primary instigator of the divide had not attended. All of us girls ended up in the same dormitory room breathing the same stale Panama City air. It was then that we realized that the things that divided us were mostly made-up and that deep down we were quite similar: silly and curious and bursting at the seams with mischief. That year we played prank after prank on each other. We hid each other's clothes and hung each other's underwear from the bedroom ceiling. The other girls, in tandem with our dorm room chaperone, the coolest of the youth group leaders' wives, hid my favorite stuffed animal. We laughed until our sides hurt and kept laughing even when our antics resulted in all of us getting a talking to.

I went to church camp every summer after moving to the new house and once I joined the youth choir and ensemble that also meant summer mission trips, once to New York and another to Louisiana. We'd sing at other churches or in parks in New York City or walk around picking up cigarette butts and trash on the streets of New Orleans, while the unrelenting sun turned all our skin shades and shades darker and the boys complained about chaffing in their jeans. We mocked the choir director's wife who warned us seriously not to interact with any of the tarot or fortune teller vendors with their booths or tables nestled in dark alleyways. We were trouble makers in the most innocent of ways and it was always our group being told off, not that we minded. We stayed up too late and giggled too loudly. We orchestrated secret bible studies late at night after the chaperones had gone to sleep. The younger girls would rap on our door quietly and we'd usher them in. For us night time bible study really meant dance parties where we twerked illicitly to music that had no business on a church trip or talked about the things the grown ups had no business interfering in. I felt extraordinarily lucky that when the trips ended and we returned home, my church friends lived so close to the new home that I saw them frequently. I spent many nights in their houses, spread out in bonus rooms eating snacks or watching movies, and yes, sometimes having actual bible studies where we contemplated God and life and held each other accountable to memorize scripture. And of course, plenty of the other kind of bible studies too.

I am telling you all this so that you understand that in some ways this new home afforded me a more spacious and relaxed existence. I was still the most myself when I was away from home. That is when my mischief and playfulness would come forward. But even at the house, there was safety in the physical sense. I still had my anxieties and dread about returning to the house at the end of the school day, just for different reasons. I no longer had to fear the threat of my body suddenly being treated as an instrument while hands or objects came steadily into contact with it and I was grateful for that. At the house I had a room and bathroom to myself. The little girl's room was across the hallway and after school and homework, I continued to play pretend with her. We turned her bedroom into another world and escaped into it for a little while, writing stories about experiences we were both famished for. I had the feeling that before I arrived she had been lonely in a way that she could not yet put into words. It was the way that she clung to me that gave it away. It was the way that I felt that in her world I was more than sister and maybe a little more like another mother or father or a mixture of both. I saw the way she needed to be tended to with a mixture of nurture and sternness. And so on those long evenings when she would come apart at the seams, crying relentlessly while protesting having to do her homework, it was me who first ushered her into my lap and soothed her and after the tears had fallen, it was me who sat at the table with her until the last of the homework was complete.

We spent the sticky Atlanta summers together in that house or running around outside, me in charge while the mother and father worked. She would wake up with her fingers tangled until almost blue in her silky blonde hair. I'd shake my head and set to work to decipher the puzzle of strands until with a sigh, I could finally release the trapped appendage. With her I, too, was an organ tangled inside strands of confusion and at times resentment. It was exhausting to shoulder the weight of additional responsibility when I myself was desperate for someone to pull me into their lap while the tears fell. I was already so weighed down, you understand me, but I had also become aware that there was not room for me to complain or need much emotionally within this new world. Gratitude was the new currency and besides all that, I really did love her. And so strand by strand I untangled myself daily from the resentment and confusion and reminded myself it was not her fault that she needed me so much. It was not her fault that she did not understand how it stung when she laughed and made a song about how much smaller my bedroom was than hers when we all moved to a new house a few years later. It was not her fault that a mural was painted to decorate her walls while my bedroom remained unfinished and without a headboard. It was not her fault that I needed to mother her while needing so desperately to be mothered myself. Strand by strand just like that until with a final sigh, I released myself to resume loving her.

I was sixteen when the wife's belly began to swell. At this point, after court dates had failed to materialize into a return to Mum's custody, and after she had signed the papers to terminate her rights to me, it was decided that my placement with the new family would be more longterm, but we will get to that later. Inside her grew a little boy who came bursting into the world when the air was crisp and the ground was still littered with leaves, like Autumn snow. They had wanted another baby for a long time and so his birth was miraculous for everyone, although mildly complicated for me. That was the way it always felt, like everyone around me seemed to be having a straightforward experience while I sat alone in a storm of confusion. Maybe deep down I had been wishing I could have been the miraculous child they had waited longingly for.

I loved him instantly. His chunky roly poly body and his blue eyes set inside his inflated cheeks made my heart swell with affection and something else. When the mother went back to work in the afternoons, he'd join the sister and I's after school antics. I pressed his little bean body near my chest while my oversized hoop earring hung low to tickle his cheek. I wondered as I looked into his little face if anyone had ever looked at me with such adoration, as their eyes became little ponds to hold the building emotion. I felt so soft toward him though it also made parts of me seize with unspent grief. I can feel it now, shimmying up and seizing me in the center of the throat.

Being the other sibling in this family was at once great joy and tremendous sorrow. I loved the children entirely. They called me their sister but years later when the older one had grown into a little adult, she said to me that when I had left for college at nineteen, she had felt abandoned by me. Not like a sister going off to school, but like a mother leaving her baby and walking out the door. We sat on the phone while the silence stretched out between us after she said the words. We talked like this often she and I, as she turned the ages I had been when we lived in the same house, as the dawning sprouted for her about what I had been tasked with and endured. She admitted sometimes in whispers that she had never seen me as a child in those days, though I was only fourteen when we met each other. The truth is I hadn't seen myself as a child back then or ever and so when she apologized and thanked me, I told her that it wasn't her job. The validation felt like a relief but the apology wasn't hers to give. It wasn't her fault though she was part of it. Being their sister meant I always had two mirrors to compare my experience against. I didn't have words for the turmoil that felt like it was eating me alive. The absolute loneliness of having a singular experience no one around me could relate to. Everyone seemed to have written my experience for me and from the outside looking only at the veneer, everything was as it should be. But no one was asking me how I was actually doing or feeling. For me it was incredibly lonely to constantly feel that I was loved but not in the same way, wanted but not like they were. I compared myself to them every day. I counted their cuddles and kisses. Every minute watching how they were treated or greeted or what they were given and what sacrifices were willing to be made in order to make sure that they had what they needed. It makes my stomach hurt, the nakedness of being so isolated in an experience nobody else was having. Some days when the comparing had knotted itself so tightly inside every part of me, I would work up the courage to ask about why it was that the other kids seemed to get more presents than I did. It is perhaps why the husband was so convinced that all I wanted was their money. But it was not about money at all. What that little baby was really saying was: am I equal? The question was about things but it was emerging from some very little and tender place, some vulnerable and shaky space and it was being asked with a trembling voice that was saying or pleading, rather:

CAN I BE EQUAL?
    can I be equal in love?
    can I be equal in dignity?
    can I be equal in belonging?
    can I be flesh and bones instead of parcel?
    a being instead of a thing that announces to the world
    on your behalf

look how good I am and charitable?

FOR ME IT was never about the things and the stuff. It was just me trying to be bridge the gap between them and me. It was about a desperate clawing and longing to be theirs like the others were. To be someone's. To feel clothed in dignity instead of undressed of equity, do you understand me? I was trying to send a signal, to shoot a flare into our shared atmosphere, but instead that signal was weaponized. I felt at times shackled to the awareness that they had opened up their home to help me out of a bad situation. Like I was chained to a post and there was only so far I could move or reach and only so much I could expect. I could not want more because I was indebted to these people from the very beginning. I entered in indebted so how dare I want more? I was supposed to be content that they fed and clothed the body even though the soul was left starving and undressed. I am a battle within myself as I type this because there is a part that still believes it is selfish to have wanted more. To have wanted to be equal because they did not owe me that, did they? I was not their daughter after all. I want to rescue them here. Or maybe I want to rescue myself from having to feel it again. To feel that teenager in me again who felt so desperate for something she could never have and felt unentitled to.

JOURNAL ENTRY

It's as if I have to pretend everything is okay. Sometimes I just want to scream. Sometimes I just want to disappear — see who in the world would even notice I were gone.

I'm tired.

The little girl doesn't even think of me as her sister anymore.

Lately she has been calling me "the babysitter"

I wonder why

She and the husband had a daddy/daughter date the other night. These people call me daughter but—

If it were a daddy/daughter night, shouldn't I have been invited?

ADOPTEE'S SOLILOQUY

How do I learn to speak when gratitude
    has been a gag order
    like a patchwork of cheesecloth clogging the throat
    a selective straining that
    allows what is easy to flow through
    yet renouncing the rest as unwanted
    waste

How do I pause the self rejection
    and dislodge the block
    permiss the whole truth to come forward
    when I have been complicit in building the narrative
    rejecting the self in order to maintain
    the veneer of belonging and of being
    Rescued

I have existed in half truths
    but now wonder if a partial existence is an existence
    that is worth preserving something that failed to
    preserve and protect my integrity
    in the end—

Perhaps becoming a home unto every piece of myself
    is a better form of belonging
    than continuing to hold myself in
    fragments
    in order to claim a family
    and in order to have a home
    in a place that only claimed the parts of me
    that enhanced their appearance
    [unintentionally?] demeaning my personhood into
    a mere commodity
    yet keeping me hidden in all the ways

I needed to be seen

Maybe for the sake of myself
    and the sake of the truth
    gratitude and wholeness can coexist
    but in order to hold them together I must take the risk
    of embracing the nakedness and loneliness of
    unbelonging and of being
    unbonded
    of being perceived, by some, as ungrateful
    that I would rather be alone than in pieces
    Maybe for the sake of myself I must
    Reach inside and dismantle the block
    unswallow to set myself free
    redignify what was treated as waste
    and in doing so unimprison the uncomfortable truth:

I am grateful and I deserved better
    I am grateful and I deserved more
    I am grateful and I deserved wholeness
    I am grateful and I deserved protection
    I am grateful and I deserved to be seen

I am grateful and I emancipate myself from a system
    that only wanted to hold me in pieces

I am grateful and I choose me

In their defense they likely got a lot more with me than they bargained for. When, on that day, German teacher had made her pleas on our behalf, and the husband's heart had been stirred and his lips had uttered some words to the wife that would change their world forever, they probably did not know what they were saying yes to. I understand that the yes had been a temporary one and that their house was only meant to be a pit stop on the way back to mum. It is what I had hoped for as well. I had hoped for reconciliation or whatever word the court was using. But none of that materialized.

At first there were court dates and plans outlined for mum in order to regain custody. I will not speak in place of her here because I was not made privy to what the plans were nor was I aware of her response to what was being asked of her. On my end I just kept petitioning social worker to please ask her to hand over my daddy's contact information and also the photo albums from my childhood. Baby sister did make it to her friend's house and so the bones of the initial plan seemed to take shape. We had our visits and it was nice to have her close by and to know that she was somewhere safe. All of that came to an abrupt end when, one day during school, social worker pulled me out of class and there was baby sister in the parking lot. She was screaming and crying and clinging onto me while I was trying to put the pieces of what was happening together. Social worker and the friend's mom were telling me that baby sister was being removed from her friend's family home. They were telling me that baby sister had been hoarding food and having some behavioral issues. I wish I had the training I have now so that I could have told them that hoarding food and behavioral issues were in line with a trauma response but I didn't know. I didn't know. And I suppose they didn't either. I felt like I was standing still while the entire earth was spinning around me. I wanted to pass out. I wanted to lay down on the concrete and go to sleep. Baby sister was there begging with trembling voice and I found myself suddenly crying out too while pleading for the family not to do this. Please don't do this, I was saying. Baby sister's cries and mine were making a desperate song that was filling up the school parking lot but it wasn't making any difference. That goodbye feels violent in my mind's eye. I felt so helpless while the car drove away. The shock was making my body rigid while my eyes kept leaking tears onto my chest. I wanted to run after the moving vehicle. I wanted to fast forward so that I was a grown up and she could come and make a home with me. I would have taken her.

After that I found it difficult to look the friend's family in the eyes when I would run into them at church. I could not do it. I did not want them to look at me or speak to me as if that moment never happened. It is because every time I saw their faces my mind floated back to that moment in the parking lot and watching my eight year old baby sister begging not to be let go. Every time I saw them my heart felt like it was being squeezed inside a fist and depleted of oxygen. The loss of that moment was not singular. It stretched on and on and on. After that baby sister returned to mum's custody. To a world that had been unbearable and now she was all alone inside it. After that communication was sparse and at times non existent between us. I did not know how to forgive them for that.

Big sister never did make it to German teacher's house. That is the way with the system, I suppose. There are plans and then there is the reality and we all made the choices we did or had certain choices imposed upon us in order to stay alive. In an instant our ties to each other seemed severed or at least changed forever, as our lives started hurtling forward on different train tracks, tracks that seemed hardly to intersect. We made our narratives about each other in order to make sense of our differences and it was not until years and years later that big sister and I had the chance to level with each other and begin to tell the truth about what we had each experienced when our worlds felt so separate. I will not tell baby sister or big sister's stories of the aftermath here. Those are their words to share. Personally I felt that I was stripped so quickly of my lineage, my ties to a line that predated my little body making its entrance into the world. It was confusing to at once have felt it dangerous to continue living with mum and yet to have felt so desperate for the sense of home that came with being in proximity to my own people and my own blood. For years Mum did not tell any of the extended family that we had been removed from her custody. They continued to call and she spun her stories that kept the truth from ever reaching their ears. For years, in the vacuum created by the silence, I believed they all knew and did not bother to come and intervene, or perhaps tuck us beside them on an airplane and fly us home and back to where it all started. To where it could have started again. I felt I was disposable. Entirely forgettable.

When, years later, some of our extended family, now living in the United States, finally found big sister on facebook, when after a missed call and a returned one, Great Aunt's voice was there on the other end of the line, I did not know what to feel. I did not know how to process that sound climbing into my ears that felt at once entirely familiar and completely foreign. So much time had passed and so much pain was taking up space inside my body that it felt that voice might cause me to splinter entirely. I wanted to run into it with limbs flailing and I wanted to turn away from it at the same time. For a while I did a bit of both, having to relearn to be in some kind of relationship with people I had felt entirely abandoned by. They did not know, Great Aunt told me persistently. I believed her but the pain and skepticism would not move so easily. I was angry and devastated. I wanted to know why they had not fought harder to get us back. Why had no one boarded a plane and pounded their fists on Mum's door, kept banging until she opened up and then demanded to know where we were. Why had they simply believed her stories? I couldn't understand it.

Great Aunt was always a devout Christian. She believed firmly in reconciliation and in forgiveness. Sometimes on our phone calls she would tell me that I should go to Mum's house and ask her for forgiveness in order for us to reconcile. The words left me one half helpless whimper and one half boiling rage. I could not believe what I was hearing her say. How were we still having the same type of conversations? I felt transported, all the way back to that day when the cherries had lead to a twisted form of torture disguised as a feast. When Great Aunt had called and instead of chastising Mum for her behavior had instead instructed us to go and make ourselves like animals at her feet and ask for forgiveness. I wanted to bellow into the phone that she was part of the problem, that her words made her complicit to everything that went on. To everything that was still going on. She was saying with one half of her words how much she has missed me, how hard it had been to be disconnected for so long, and with the other half of her words she was telling me that my safety did not matter to her at all. I didn't understand how she was not seeing it and truthfully I was tired of this version of love.

I went silent after that. I watched her name light up the screen of my cell phone and I let it ring until I knew she was hearing the recording of my voice on the other side. I couldn't decide what felt worse, the complete disconnection or the type of connection that lacked protection. She told me later, after months and months of calls left unanswered and unreturned by me, it had caused her to go into a state of panic and fear.

"I was afraid I had lost you again," she said with emotion clogging her throat.

I could hear the toll those years we had been lost from each other had taken on her. It felt like a relief to know that maybe someone had been longing for me all along. I had a twin desire to be close that matched hers but I told her that I would not have conversations about going to ask for forgiveness anymore. If she wanted a relationship, we just had to leave Mum out of it entirely. I was only willing to have a relationship with the half of her that had missed me. The other half had to stay out of it. It was the only way I knew to do it. I was tired of no one ever seeming to hold the perpetrators accountable for anything, but I also didn't have the energy to fight with Great Aunt over concepts like forgiveness either. The truth is that by the time great aunt was whispering those words into my ear, I had already written Mum a lengthy letter. In it I had tried to convey the reasons why we left and at the end I did type out an ask for forgiveness if there had been something I had done to deserve that kind of treat-ment. I was nineteen at the time, four years after that day we left home. With that letter I had already bent myself to my knees in front of her one more time. I had done it because I was sick with the heartache of knowing that both my sisters were in contact with her, though she had never made any attempt at communication with me. I had typed out the words to that letter in between college classes while my vision was going blurry from tears and my fingers were shaking as they slid across the keyboard. I was desperate to understand why she had discarded me like trash. What had to be true about me that she was able to carve me out of her heart so easily, though once I was little enough to fit inside her body, dependent entirely on her for survival. I know she received that letter because baby sister told me as much, but from Mum herself there was never any acknowledgment. Her silence left me awash in currents of self hatred. I hated that I'd sent the letter, handing her the power one more time by revealing to her how desperate I was for her affection. I wished I was stronger. I didn't want to crave her love but it felt impossible not to. After all these years I was still so desperate for her approval. It always felt to me that Mum was aware that her silence, that her complete rejection of me would hurt me more than anything else. More than shoe or spoon or fist on flesh, and she was right as well. Rejection seemed always to surround me and with it those age old lies I had ingested from as young as I can remember,

"You are worthless," said the voice that was meant to soothe, swimming in my head like a song on repeat and, "no one will ever love you."

I believed it entirely. There was just something about me in particular, I'd tell myself and the belief only seemed to deepen within this new world in which, no matter how much a I tried to be as easy as possible, I never could find a way to be loved with equity.

BONDAGE

It feels like bondage when the only proof of you
    lies in the hands of the person
    who tried to beat the humanity out of you.
    It feels like bondage
    when all the untold stories are buried in the ground,
    being eaten away by nature's rhythms,
    now just hollow bones that cannot speak.
    It feels like bondage when the pain is not visible,
    and when the stories are sewn into pockets of flesh
    on the inside of you that no one can see.
    It feels like bondage to wait and wonder and wish
    for things you can't get back.
    You simply cannot get them back;
    you never had them to start with.
    It feels like bondage to be alive
    and somehow feel lifeless at the same time.
    It feels like bondage to know that the mourning is necessary,
    when the mourning feels
    like the biggest bondage of all.

Forgive me, what I was trying to say here is that the new family probably got a lot more than they had bargained for with me. By the time it became obvious that the court dates would not lead to reconciliation and when mum signed the papers to terminate her rights as parent, then the husband and wife had a conversation and decided I could stay long term. I don't know how that conversation went or what was said or if there was any hesitation. I was not there to push them or beg them, they decided entirely on their own. It feels important for me to say it because at times I felt I was being punished for being in their house. It was not my decision. In any case I can imagine what a disruption to their timeline I was. It was, I imagine, quite a leap to go from learning to parent a toddler to suddenly having a traumatized teenager sleeping inside their home, and a black child at that. Maybe we were all going to sleep with a little bit of whiplash during those years. I think this is where the system fails everyone. For a long time I was furious with the husband and wife for not parenting the part of me that was contemplating death. I was furious that they never put me inside their lap and rocked me while I wept from the impact of everything that life had been up to this point and what life continued to be. That they did not offer to stay awake beside me and keep watch so that I could sleep. All I wanted was for someone to let me be little for a while, to let the seams burst open and to witness everything that might pour out of me. Yet another part of me now wonders if I can blame them entirely. Maybe they needed to be parented by the system in order to know how to parent me. Maybe they needed a functioning system to put them in its lap so that they would know how to do that for me, I don't know. Because the training isn't adequate and so maybe we were in some ways mirror images and the ways I felt missed and neglected reflected the ways the system had missed and neglected them as well. It still hurt me but no one was helping them either. No one was coming beside them and holding their hands so that they would know how to make themselves an open space for me to come apart in. No one was saying check on her, even though she seems okay, you should still check on her sometimes. No one was telling them how to look beyond the surface and recognize the signs of PTSD. No one was telling them they should go to their own therapy to manage this sudden twist in their own reality so that they did not project it on me. No one was checking on them to see how all of it was impacting them and so we all just existed in the vortex of unmet needs and unprocessed trauma, ping ponging off each other painfully. I did my best to offer them the pretend version of me and is it their fault they bought it? Is it their fault that on the outside I appeared highly functional and well adjusted while I suffered silently? I'd honed my pretend skills quite well by this point, so is it their fault that they didn't prod beyond the exterior? I can't be sure.

For the most part my relationship with the mother was good. She was full of warmth and kindness and we had our moments of laughing together until our bellies hurt. I did feel loved by her and even wanted in ways. Her complacency often frustrated me, leaving me feeling unprotected and ultimately uncared for, but passivity, at the time, felt like the lessor of the evils and at least she was consistent. I will always take a constant variable over one that is always changing. She was good to me and so I let the ways that she didn't protect me fall away for a while. She was softer with me than most people had been and that counted for something. It counted for a lot. She was soft with me even when, early on in my stay there, my newly found obsession with pornography corrupted the family computer. Even then she was soft with me. She sat me down and asked me what was happening. My heart was convulsing inside my chest and I was sure I had just made the type of error that would terminate my placement in that house. I told her with tears rolling down my face that I just wanted to feel something. I don't think she understood what I was saying because I hardly did, but she hugged me after and that was the end of it.

As the weeks passed by our relationship blossomed into something that felt more like friendship than anything else. She felt very much like a young soul living inside of a body two decades older than mine and so most times she felt more like a peer than a parent and when we were having fun I didn't mind it. She really was a fun friend to have, young in ways that made her somewhat relatable. We baked cookies and went shopping and watched American Idol and So You Think You Can Dance, letting our eyes well with emotion at the impassioned performances. We went on shopping trips to her favorite boutiques. Together we'd scour the racks and fill our arms up with dresses and jumpsuit for her to slip into in the changing room. I cheered from the sidelines and told her how beautiful she looked in every item and when we reached the register at the end of the afternoon, I vowed to keep secret the money she was charging to the credit card the husband was not aware of.

For me the best nights were the ones when the husband was away traveling for work. The best nights were ordering expensive sushi and nestling together in front of the television while I swooned over David Cook on the screen. It is funny isn't it - how in the first part of life, safety only came with the presence of a father and in the second part, the absence of a father. But that was the truth. When he wasn't home I at least did not have to spend so much energy being overly aware of his shape shifting moods and it was one less thing to have to regulate. I don't think I would be lying to say we all felt it, but I will only speak for myself. I liked her best when it was just the two of us. Like the night we went to the movies and being unable to decide whether to see 13 Going on 30 or The Prince and Me, saw both back to back while shoving candy in our mouths and sharing swoons over Mark Ruffalo. It was Cookie Dough Bites for her and Skittles for me. I felt like we were both hormonal teenagers that night, hearts bursting and giggles erupting endlessly. Or the time we took a trip, just the two of us, to New York City. I was obsessed with the Phantom of the Opera at the time. I could relate to the Phantom's darkness and disfigured frame, although my own scars were hidden from the naked eye. I could relate to the feeling of being rejected from birth. The wife bought us front row tickets to the show as a graduation gift to me. I remember when I opened the sealed envelope. I remember how as my eyes focused to turn the letters printed on the tickets into words, a squeal burst out of my body to fill up the kitchen. I remember next the devastation I felt when we missed our flight and how by the time we landed in New York and took a taxi to the theatre, the show was completely over. I broke down in tears right there in the lobby with the security guard watching my unexpected performance. He told us to wait while he went to get the director of the show. After he heard our story he told us to come back the next night and he would make sure we had seats. The next night, after we had dressed in our fancy clothes and after we ate dinner at a quaint Italian Restaurant where the waiter serenaded us with words I did not understand and yet brought tears to my eyes, then we returned to the scene of the previous night's disappointment. We walked to the will call and told them our names. We gasped in delight when we were told that the director had reserved two seats in his box for us to sit in. I sat beside the wife that night basking in the pure magic that had been recycled from a potentially disheartening moment. I let the music swallow me up entirely and when the voice of the Phantom boomed from some-where up in the balcony, I wondered what it might be like to exit my seat and disappear into the night with him. The wife squeezed my hand when my eyes began leaking tears, both of us touched, moved, entirely overwhelmed by the sheer magic of the moment.

My relationship with the husband would best be described a complicated. I am trying as I write this to imagine holding the thread between him and me in the palm of my hands. I am trying to ask my mind to trace and retrace the strand of our relationship so that I can try to identify what things were like before the tension, but I cannot seem to remember. It had not alway been strained between us, surely. Maybe it had been the stress of my permanency? Or maybe his own trauma recognized a kinship in me and by rejecting me he was really rejecting a piece of himself? I really don't know. I don't remember the beginning feeling so forceful between us and yet, I can't seem to remember him in the beginning at all. Not on my first weeks in that house when we were all operating under the impression that I was only there temporarily. I don't remember if he had been sweet or soft with me then. I am trying to remember because I am not trying to paint anyone as a unilateral being here. I do believe there is a sweetness in him, I just can't remember if I was ever a recipient of it. When I think of him it all feels like such a shame really. Beyond the tension there could have been so much to connect on. We are so alike in some ways. We are both adventurers deep down, I think. We both enjoy trying new food and traveling and being outdoors. The wife would have been content with Disney World and Chick-Fil-A for a lifetime but I think the two of us may have enjoyed dreaming up alternate adventures. But by the time the tension came, we could not seem to make room for our similarities. By the time the tension came, I doubled down to reject any notion of proximity to him. I did not know how to be soft enough to let us be similar yet hard enough to keep myself protected from him.

For a while he traveled sometimes three out of five days of the work week. When he got home, when the lights of his truck illuminated the front windows, my insides started doing some sort of peculiar gyration. As soon as his feet crossed the threshold, I experienced the house as suddenly overcrowded, like there was one too many of us fighting for breathing room. When he was away I had the feeling that I had more space, or more of a place, rather. I could play the role of surrogate parent, sister and partner and any other roles I felt was implicitly expected of me while keeping my straight As and myself regulated enough so that I did not attempt suicide. When he got home, it felt like the daughter and the mother still needed me to take care of things, and at the same time it felt like he would blow up in rage that I was occupying a space he felt should have been his. He was right, of course, it should have been his. But I felt I was being looked to to somehow hold this world together and I didn't know what to do. How to find that perfect amount of space I should occupy where I was being useful without stepping on his toes or his need for authority. It all felt so familiar. All I wanted was for someone to mark the lines plainly or to hand me a manual but unfortunately the parents I had inherited in this life did not come with one and so I was left to do my best to dodge the invisible landmines.

He seemed always to be pregnant with aggression and it was never clear what or who would be the catalyst for him to birth all that rage and invite it full force into the house. It could be anything. When he was home, we would nestle in front of the television, as we did while he was away, and in he would march and without a word change the channel on the television. If anyone protested, he would point at the television and say,

"Who paid for that television?" and proceed to change the channel.

I found his behavior difficult to respect. It disgusted and enraged me. I hated the way he talked to the wife and the way he held his role of primary financial provider over her like a weapon, as if because he made more money he was entitled to more power and control. Since no one else was doing it, I would open my mouth and challenge him, telling him I didn't like the way he talked to the her or any of us. I glared at him when once in anger, he picked the little girl up by the arm and waved her around in the air like a rag doll. I don't remember the reaction the mother had while her baby was lifted into the air so carelessly and with force. The contempt was probably etched into the lines in my forehead and the fire radiating out of my eyeballs before any words came tumbling out of my mouth for him to stop.

Whenever the rage was climbing out of his body, the little girl would run into my arms and I would comfort her or we would disappear into her bedroom until it blew over. I hated the way his voice box would at times become a stereo speaker, broadcasting on a loop that all I wanted was their money and that I was ungrateful. Those times I would make my face a blank canvas. I would make myself unaffected because I did not want to hand him the satisfaction of knowing the way his words were rattling my insides, shaking me about as if I was the body suspended in the air by his arm. I didn't want him to know that every time the word ungrateful left his mouth, it left me feeling like nothing even though I was trying so hard to become something to him. I would deal with the sting later when the house was sleeping and I was lying alone in the darkness, but standing there in front of him, I would not soften.

Conceivably you are wondering about the sudden change in me, how I metamorphosed from the terrified girl in the start of this story into this version who could remain unflinching in the face of threat. I understand. Let me explain. The terror had not dissolved. It had not evaporated into thin air even though I could somehow convince the exterior to appear unflinching. The truth is I had been unloaded into a new landscape and ecosystem in which everyone else's strategy seemed to be to fold and freeze in the face of this particular threat. I did not feel I got a say as to which role I played and so I adopted the role of protector since it seemed to be the one that was vacant upon my arrival. It meant going head to head with the threat even though inside my body was awash with tremors of fear and even though the husband's resemblance to Mum was making parts of me bang around inside my body like they were trying to wake me up from a bad dream. It meant making myself a stone even though the words he chose were like knives pressing painfully against wounds that were still festering and oozing, cutting new lesions on top of skin that was already lacerated. I felt sometimes entirely convinced that Mum must visit him in the night and deposit into his ears the exact words to say that would upset my internal equilibrium the most.

With him I felt I was always on edge. I was terrified that he would kick me out of the house. I was terrified that he was confirming all the things Mum had said were true about me. I was terrified that his rage might turn physical, and maybe in some ways I would have preferred it to the way his words felt like sandpaper rubbing against the remaining shreds of my positive sense of self. I stood there and made my body rigid but inside I was just a little girl looking up at yet another grown up who could not seem to love me and who could not seem to soften. Inside I was a sheep but on the outside, life demanded the wolf to come forward, you understand me?

Sometimes when things were bad between the husband and I, the wife would tell me that he had experienced trauma as a child. Maybe she said it to keep the empathy inside me alive or maybe to make him more relatable to me. I wanted to scream at her to stop having grown up conversations with me, to try and soften me toward him and instead go into her bedroom and hold him accountable or get him to be the one to bear the weight of softening. I didn't know why it had to be my responsibility. Why was everything on me? Truthfully, I did want to connect with him. Deep down I wanted the skeletons of his trauma to reach across to the skeletons of mine and the two become friends. I would at times muster up some strength, convince my heart to open a little. I'd talk myself into looking him in the eye and approaching him with softness. He would at times soften back. He'd insist we go out to eat just the two of us and I had enough sense not to protest. I did not enjoy being one on one with him. It felt very much like going to pick up dinner with mum on my birthday. That feeling of being so anxious I wanted to come out of my skin. I really tried to will my body to relax but it felt difficult. Impossible, even. I never knew which version of him I was about to get and the two versions were so drastically different that I felt I always had to be prepared. Sometimes time alone would only expand the canyon between us as we went head to head. Other times he would, at the end of our dinners, pull over into a secluded parking lot and look me in the eyes while he shed some tears at the awareness he was carrying about not being a "good father" and of "failing me." I'd pat him on the back and hold the edges so he could come undone and absolve himself. He never asked me in those moments what it was like for me. He was never curious about my experience nor did he offer to return the favor and hold the edges so that I could release some of the emotion pent up inside me. Those moments were about us but they were for him, do you understand me? No one patted me on the back to soothe the ache of his failings. I'd tell him it was okay. I said it because I just wanted it to be over and for us to get back to the house as quickly as possible so I could go to my room. I knew this man was the biggest split screen I had encountered yet. Like my daddy, he seemed to have a few different souls inside of his body but they felt so dissonant from each other I really didn't know if they knew the others existed. That is why I could not let his softness land inside my body and curate any

feelings of hope. His softness and his awareness were always temporary. The husband would cry when his heart caught up with the rest
of him and then shortly after we would be right back in the loop. One
minute he was soft and the next minute dangerous. One minute in
despair for the way he was failing and the next calling me incompetent for crying about the pain of my own experience. It felt familiar
but that didn't mean I didn't feel the fatigue of all of it eating away at
me slowly.

One Sunday when the wife was out of town, when it was just me
and the little girl and the baby brother, us children woke up and the
husband was still nestled away inside his bedroom. I thought maybe
he had decided we would not go to church that day and so I didn't
bother to get the little ones ready. We sat, instead, watching cartoons
in front of the television, the little girl twirling her fingers in her hair
as she always did and the baby brother sitting in my lap, a contented
little lump munching on cereal. I heard him coming down the stairs. I
was still in the business of memorizing the meaning of different
sounds and so I could tell by the way that his feet were hitting the
wooden stairs that he was wearing his church shoes. I waited
anxiously for him to appear. When he asked why we were not dressed
I said I didn't know that we were going since he had not been awake.
He said we should get ready so that we could go to the second service.
I took the girl and the boy upstairs to get them dressed. The little boy
hid under the ping pong table because he wasn't interested in this
sudden interruption to his Sunday morning cartoons. I heard the
husband's feet carrying him up the stairs and toward the playroom
where the little boy was hiding. The husband's impatience exploded
out of his body like lightening leaving a cloud. The room seemed to be
shaking like a thunderous reply. I kneeled down and made my voice a
whisper to try and gently coax the little boy out of hiding. Something
about that action set the husband off. That was how it was, blink and
you could return to an entirely different reality.

"They are my children and I will get them ready!" he screeched.

Clearly he felt I had undermined his authority. It had not been my
intention but I didn't bother to argue and instead descended the stairs

to begin getting dressed, leaving him to attend to his own children. Impatience was flowing hot inside my own body. I could hear his voice booming and breath huffing not far behind me as he followed me downstairs and banged my bedroom door open. My senses were already standing at attention. With my back turned I swallowed in one big breath of air to ready myself for a fight I had accidentally initiated. Once inside the room he started screaming at me and banging his hands against the wall. My insides were vibrating with that familiar sensation that feels like someone has your heart in a chokehold. Everything in my periphery blurred away and all that was left was his frame in front of me. He was playing his hands against the wall like he was banging on a drum and screaming at me that I was ungrateful, that I thought of them as just money bags. All I wanted was their money, he was saying, while his body was inching closer and closer to mine. My heart was trying again to evict itself from my chest. I felt he was trying to break me, like he was working hard to frighten me into bending to him, perhaps sliding down onto my knees in submission like I had done for years in front of Mum. On the outside you may have seen my face and body still like a statue, but inside I was torn in two parts, each one screaming and warring with the other on what I should do next. One was saying, just give in. Just tell him you are sorry and agree, bend, break, do whatever it takes to make it stop. The whole room was vibrating in warning, like the sound a shoe makes as it soars backwards before it connects with flesh. But my knees would not bend like they used to because another voice was now living inside me. It was the wolf and with a boom she was saying haven't you had enough, girl? And truthfully I had. I had had enough. I'd had enough of being screamed at and belittled and backed into a corner while someone bigger than me and with more power pressed all that power up against my body and bent me to my knees. I'd had enough of managing landmines and changeable moods. I'd had enough of having my dignity shredded. I'd had enough so I didn't move. I didn't move and instead asked my face to be a stone while we stood there face to face, his skin now the hue of an overripe tomato. I looked at him, willing my features to remain blank just a little longer. And then out from my lips, more steadily than I felt inside,

"Listen to me - I have already done this one time in my life. I have already been beaten and I have already been screamed at and I am not doing it again. I am not doing it again. If you want me to go then just say so. If you don't want me here then just say that and I will go, but I am not doing this again."

It was my lips that had formed the words and still the words stunned me. I knew I was playing with fire. I could feel the energy between us cresting and cresting and I knew that the end of the line might be flesh against flesh and then a ripple. I knew but I didn't care. If he hit me I wanted him to do it while I looked him in the eyes so that he could see himself while he did it. The tears were threatening to crawl up and out of my eyes but I kept them back. I was enraged and terrified, unsure what would become of this new variable I had welcomed into the room. His words had bruised the surface of my heart but I would not show him. My chest was heaving and my ears were ringing and ringing. It was my eyes that were looking at him squarely but the truth is most of me was watching from above. Floating.

He did not back down and continued his rampage. He banged his hand one last time against the door, not seeing that the little boy was standing there on the other side of the threshold. The bottom of the door caught the edge of the little boy's foot and he was there on the floor crying while blood was trickling out of the cut that had split his skin. I was right, these things did always end with someone wailing on the floor. This time just not me. I felt a little guilty.

"Are you happy now?" I shouted wearily.

The crying must have sobered him up. It must have given his heart time to catch up to the rest of him. It must have allowed more than his rage to come into view. I guess I will give him credit for that much. He bent to his knees to tend to the little boy and I used that little pothole in time to shove some clothes into a bag. I put my shoes on and I walked out the door. The rain was coming down violently that day. It was falling hard against my body and making my jeans heavy against my legs, but I kept on moving. My feet were taking a swim in puddles along the street and I wished they were deep enough to swallow me whole. I wished they would just swallow me up entirely. I kept walking down the street until I reached my friend's house. I rapped my knuckles on the door and when she opened collapsed there soaking the floor in a mixture of rain and tears. I let my own heart catch up with the rest of me and it was broken. It was so broken.

OPPORTUNITY

Your arms were meant to be an opportunity. They probably forgot to tell you while you signed your name
    on the line that would make me yours. Or maybe they didn't think this was pertinent information.
    After all, being your daughter was only meant to be a temporary transaction.
    I wasn't meant to become a fixture, a burden—
    as you preferred to put it.

Your arms were meant to be an opportunity. Months later, when you decided that you would keep me,
    I should have told you then that when you choose a person, you choose the entirety of them.
    Don't get me wrong, I do believe that somewhere in your head you really thought you had fully chosen.
    Inside your head you had crunched all the numbers and had concluded that there were sufficient resources to make an orphan a child, to make my presence permanent.
    You convinced yourself that your insides would also make room eventually, not immediately,
    but eventually your insides would be willing to undergo construction and create one more room.
    For me.

Your arms were meant to be an opportunity.
    A quiet hedge in which bones, already broken and re-broken,
    would finally have the opportunity to heal,
    where muscle, now ripped to shreds,
    would miraculously regenerate,
    a place for the broken heart
    to rehabilitate.
    A sanctuary, perhaps.

Your arms were meant to be an opportunity. But it probably wasn't your fault that this did not come to pass. It is in my nature, it seems, to attract the type of parent that finds me burdensome in the end.

No matter how endlessly I labor, how little space I endeavor to take up, no matter how small I try to make myself seem, I am always burdensome

in the end.

You arms were meant to be an opportunity. But your insides seemed frozen and immobilized

by some secret pain of your own. They couldn't, for unexpressed reasons, find the will to allow the bulldozers in to create that extra room.

So—instead I took up residence on the outside of your insides, palms pressed against the glass, peering in. You peered back, your eyes looking into mine as we both waited for "eventually."

And for that time when your arms would finally be:

An opportunity.

L ater when the rain had died down and when my sobs had emptied themselves out into those heavy after crying body shudders, then my cell phone rang against my pocket. It was the husband calling and I did not answer. He called again and I left it. A third time and I let it ring. After that he texted saying the little girl, my sister, wanted to talk to me. I could not turn her down and so I called. I called not for his sake but for hers.

It was his voice on the other side. To tell me that the little boy was okay and to tell me to come home for lunch. I said no. Then the little boy on the other side confirming in his soft toddler voice that he really was okay. And then finally the little girl's voice - a shaky whisper into the phone,

"If you don't come home I don't know what I'll do."

I went back. What would you have done?

My friend offered to walk me back to the house but I declined. After the little girl's voice had put the weight of preserving her safety and sanity into my ears, I needed the walk back to gather myself together. As one foot after the other dragged itself against the pavement, the tears started to spill over again. It was if I could taste the internal fatigue, metallic and earthy inside my mouth. I felt light-headed and overheated. I stopped and pressed my eyelids shut, begged and pleaded for these parts that were coming undone to go and find a home in the nameless place for a little while. I would at times have the feeling that someone or something was pumping hot air into my body and as I inflated the borders of me were straining to keep everything contained. That is the feeling I had here. But I knew I could not come undone. I knew because I understood that no one would come and put me back together. I felt so helpless. I had nowhere else to go and yet I felt my continued dependence on others like a rope tightening against my neck. All I wanted was to be grown up and independent. All I wanted was enough money to look after myself. I just wanted to be left blissfully alone. There were other thoughts that day while I walked the short distance back to the house and as the cars of neighbors drove by my slow moving frame. I was fighting with myself to keep my steps in a straight line instead of veering off in a zig zag and into the oncoming traffic.

"If you don't come home I don't know what I'll do," I let that little girl's words play inside my head and with it the image of her small face. It was the only thing that helped me make it home.

Later that afternoon when the wife returned from her trip, I was sitting at the kitchen table doing my homework. She had gone to Savannah and had brought back pralines in little green boxes. When she set them beside me I looked up at her and said with seriousness,

"Do you want me to be here or not?"

"Why are you asking me that?" she said back. I told her to go and ask the husband.

To her credit she did march quite loudly up the wooden stairs and she did slam the door when she reached their bedroom. It was one of the few times I watched her shift out of passivity and do something about what was happening in that house and I was grateful. I don't know what words were said up there. I only know that when she returned she simply pressed a kiss to my cheek and that much later the husband invited me into his office to apologize. His apology captured both parts of him very well. The one part that was, perhaps earnestly, sorry for the way he had behaved and for the things that he said, and the other part that made sure I knew that it would not have happened if I had been more grateful. I didn't have the energy to argue with him so I just waited for him to tire himself out. I wanted to ask him why I was the only child being constantly assaulted with reminders to be grateful. I wanted to ask him but I already knew the answer. I let him finish his half apology. The apology was not for me since there was no room in that conversation for my experience. It was for him. Perhaps for him to justify his own behavior and appease the wife but I did not argue.

That night, I let my mind play my life to me like a film. I shook violently while the sobs escaped my body and when the tape finished, when I was all the way caught up, I whispered into the darkness,

"I'm not their child, they don't owe me anything."

I said it over and over again to help me disengage from the pain so that I could keep going. I could keep smiling and telling the story the way I was supposed to tell it. So I could keep trying to be good and compliant and useful and grateful, the only space I was meant to occupy. I didn't understand how any of this could be happening. It sometimes felt like I was the butt of some cruel joke that the universe or God or whoever, was telling. To wander into yet another home where my mere existence seemed to trigger landmines all of the time. At night I'd fall into bed and squeeze my eyes shut. I just felt so tired. I doubted myself constantly. Maybe the husband was right and I was just ungrateful. Why couldn't I get this role as daughter right? I was trying. I was trying hard to carve the right parts of myself away. I really was trying to contain my stubbornness and sassiness so that I could just have a little bit of peace, but it never seemed like enough. I didn't actually know what else he wanted from me, if I am being honest. I felt that much of the time I was raising myself and others in that house. I woke myself up in the morning, I got myself dressed, I walked myself to the bus stop in the dark, I was never late for school, I never got into trouble. I cooked if they needed me to, babysat the children after school until the mother got home from work. I got good grades and they never had to check whether or not I had finished my school work. Some nights I stayed up late into the night finishing a project and still I did not oversleep the next morning. What else did he want from me except for me to disappear entirely? I am asking you because I still do not know the answer. After all these years I still do not have the answer. I felt like I was being punished for existing there, for taking up space. As if I had had anything to do with the decision to be there. I was grateful for a home but why take me if I was only going to be punished for being there? Constantly reminded that my presence was an inconvenience and a strain. If it was going to be so obvious that I was there but not wanted there. Or rather, if I was just an inconvenience using up their money. It always seemed to boil down to the money for him. I wanted to scream. I wanted to run. I wanted to fulfill his wish and disappear altogether. I just felt like my insides were hemorrhaging. I had been through much harder, I'd tell myself, trying hard to silence the voice that kept telling me to do something drastic. The hopes that once roared inside me would at times transform into something dark and sinister on those lonely nights when all I wanted was an open field and my daddy's chest to rest my head on. On those nights when the idea of being alive would feel heavier than the alternative.

It would slide out of me sometimes, this contemplation of death. It would slide out in poems left around the house on bright green construction paper or whatever I could find. The wife would find them and ask about the words scribbled there. I don't know what I said, maybe nothing. Eventually there were enough scraps of construction paper left around the house, like crumbs left to lead them to the place that was hurting, that they sent me to see a therapist. I credit her for helping me stay alive. For being a place where the seams could relax a little bit and let enough out so that I could keep moving. Here therapy was to stabilize the internal crisis. The actual processing of everything would not happen until much later but those months with her kept me alive.

Much much later when I realized that although I was functional, I wasn't okay, when I found myself sitting in therapy for three years as an adult, after I had processed through the trauma of the first part of life, then the therapist reflected this second family experience to me as traumatic. I looked at her in silence. I looked at her and my body began to shudder. It was part relief and part fear. She was seeing what no one was supposed to see and that scared me. She was seeing what everyone had failed to see, naming it clearly and it was the relief of being seen that turned the shudders into whimpers. With her words she was putting clothes back on some part of me that had been standing there naked and humiliated for so long but I had been naked for so long I did not know how to feel the clothing as anything but a threat. If I let myself melt into the truth I was afraid the pain might swallow me whole. I was afraid it would kill me. I shook my head while I cried. I said to her, "they don't owe me anything, I am not their daughter." I was doing what I had always done to try and stay together but she did not allow the excuse to hold up and instead gently asked me if that rule would have applied if I had chosen to bring a child into my home. She was speaking directly to the part of me that had always been maternal by nature. She asked me why I seemed to owe them an allegiance that forced me to disown the truth of my experience. She asked me because she knew that even then, while I was in therapy as an adult, when I had been processing the experiences of the first part of life, and I had called the wife reaching for a bit of comfort, she had said,

"I don't have space for this," and hadn't that always been true? Hadn't there never been space for my experience?

The therapist asked me finally if love was about owing people. I felt like vomiting on her carpet. Because the answer was no. The answer was of course, no. I probably dissociated right there and then because I did not want to face this. I did not want to hold my whole life together in my hands as I am doing now and face what was true. It felt like too much. The therapist called me back by saying my name very loudly in the quiet office while I started hyperventilating.

"I can't breathe," I was telling her.

"You can breathe," she was saying back. But I did not want to breathe. I did not want to stay in that room and face it.

JOURNAL ENTRY

What do I do with the realization that no one's ever seen me. Or maybe — that I have never let anyone ever see me. See the scared little beaten girl that lives inside me. See the attempts to cover up the wounds that still bleed. To see what lies beyond the edges of my pretty little smile.

Will anyone want me when they know how broken I can be? They hardly want me now though I try to be pristine.

Will anyone want me when they know how broken I can be? Once they see the festering side of me. The scars that never healed and the tears pleading to be set free.

TODAY:

This grief is emptying me out
    Wringing me dry
    It comes like a rock in the cavity of the chest
    A slight tickle, then a cough to announce
    The complete confinement of breath
    Before the body seizes
    Then she is there - with her body curled against the floor
    With her eyelids pressing themselves shut
    And her legs clenching tightly
    As they shake, as they violently tremble
    As if to keep out the pain that is scouring her
    Devouring her
    Making a feast of the last shreds
    Of her resistance - of her hope
    I wish I could carve the agony out of her
    Scrape it loose from the marrow of her fragile bones
    But I must be different than the others
    Lay down beside her and let what is true
    Be true
    Resist the urge to want to scrape her clean
    And make her easy, make her useful
    I won't pretend I'm not afraid
    To meet her
    To meet myself

—

I lay down
    I put my face near her face
    I make my body a companion for her
    As they should have done
    As they should have done
    I rub a palm on her back

I stroke my fingers against her face
Hold her close until
Her brown eyes peak slowly open
"Oh god," slips out from the quivering lips
I nod my head while the tears swell in our eyes
Spill over and crawl down the cheeks
As we both shake
As we groan in unison
And weep
And wail
And whimper
As we ride the wave of grief to its peak
Roar together as it crests
And breathe to feel it all together
Her small hand lifts to rest on my chest
While a timid smile curves the lips
I nod my head again
And we find ourselves falling out of grief
Falling and sailing and settling into
Something remarkably unfamiliar

—

Like this I cut the chord between love and exploitation
Between love and charity
Like this I cut myself open and show her the space that is hers
Like this I whisper, welcome home, love
As they should have done
As they should have done
Like this I offer her a love that is spacious
And a love that is free
As it should have been
As it should have been

Here I am tempted to defend myself, I want to be honest with you. I am tempted to defend myself so that you will not think of me as ungrateful. So that you will not agree with him that all I wanted was their money. It is the old conditioning because I am doing here what I have never been allowed to do. I am telling you the whole truth of my experience. But it is hard to move against all the parts of me that are straining in warning because this has not been allowed. The story I have been allowed to tell, and have told, is one about being rescued. It is the one about how a white family took in a black girl and saved her. It is the one about how they thought I needed them but they actually needed me. It is the one where love is colorblind and so I still feel so guilty for wanting more.

I am tempted to defend myself because I want you to know that I was grateful. I was grateful that I was never hungry and that I was always clothed. I was grateful for my own bedroom and my own bathroom. I was grateful that they did not only rely on the meager stipend offered to them by the Foster Care System and instead used their own money to pay for summer camp and trips to Disney World. For church choir and ensemble. I was grateful for shopping trips and for baking cookies late at night. I was grateful for Barbies in the playroom and for getting to see Usher on my 16th birthday where my gleeful screams left me without a voice the next morning. I was grateful that no one was beating me or exploring my body in the middle of the night. I was grateful and still am but all that gratitude also cost me something, do you understand me? Do you know what it is like to have to choose between safety and dignity? To choose between wholeness and having a place? Everything I did felt filtered through the lens of what they had done for me. I am not saying I was a perfect child. I was a hormonal teenager with a stubborn edge. I could have a bad attitude and I didn't like being told what to do. But none of that was able to fit underneath the umbrella of typical child development because any movement outside of the line was equated with a signal of my ingratitude. There is a particular and sometimes subtle demoralization that exists when love becomes an act of charity. All I wanted was a place where love did not feel like some sort exploitation. There was nowhere I could put this longing. No one I could tell. Because by everyone's estimation I had been rescued. Inside I still felt like I was dying. Or rather - inside I would have preferred death. I was still keeping secrets. It felt as if I was always responsible for preserving the good image of the grown ups in my life. Protecting and preserving the narrative - even if it degraded my own humanity. In High School all the students had to write an essay for the Laws of Life competition. I wrote it and my essay was chosen to represent the school. I was proud of myself even though I knew I had disowned a big part of myself and of my experience by writing the words. I wrote an essay about the way that love does not see the color of someone's skin. That is the fantasy isn't it? And I wanted it to be true. I really wanted it to be true but really, I was just telling the story that someone who is grateful tells. And the story that someone who is desperate for family tells. And in order to tell that story, I had to leave out the ways that the color of my skin, and the skin of those like me, seemed to matter very much when we drove to Alabama to see the extended family.

On every holiday and a few other times during the year, we all packed our bags and made the drive to North Alabama, where the husband and wife's family lived. I don't remember the first visit there and I don't know what the husband and wife told their families about who I was and why I was with them. The wife's father was a preacher and when, a few years later, I got into Vanderbilt, I remember his voice booming down from the pulpit of the church talking about how I, once in the foster care system, was now going to Vanderbilt. That felt like a good approximation of the standing narrative. I wanted to tell him that I had been planning to go to college on a full ride long before I met the family, but I simply nodded while we stood up and the congregation clapped. In those moments I felt more like a trophy than a child but with all the eyes in the room settling on me and them and as I stood there like one lonesome freckle painted against a sea of porcelain, I just smiled compliantly.

Alabama was the birthplace of their love story, years and years before our meeting when their faces were still smooth and untouched by age. She had been the quintessential southern girl, with her twangy accent and manicured hair, full and fluffy to fit the decade perfectly. I am blank on who he was then. I have no descriptors to write about him here but anyway, they met each other and we can just call the rest history. Later when the husband and the wife moved the three hours away to Atlanta they may have been considered brave or even rebellious since their hometowns felt like one of those places where everyone seemed to stay put.

In Alabama was the wife's mom and dad, her brother, and her sister and her family. The husband's dad and step mom, while she was still living, were less than a half hour away and a little farther than that, his mom. We shuffled between the houses, either spending the night at the wife's parents' house or at the husband's dad's house, before tacking on a visit to his mom's house usually at the end of the trip. There were merits to each of the houses, though probably hardest to identify at the husband's mom's house. On the drive to her small home my eyes greeted cows contained behind fences and my nose twitched as the smell of manure snuck in through the car's air conditioning to perfume the entire space. The smell was unpleasant but it also transported me all the way back to the farm in Africa. All the way back to those years when Daddy had decided to build a large chicken coop in the back of our property. It was a similar smell then, as big sister and I braved the stench to go and hold the little chicks like babies in the palm of our hands while we offered them unique names though they all looked the same.

At the husband's mom's house the discomfort was physical. The house was dirty and I found it hard to find a corner to sit on that was free from dust or dirt. The little girl and I would sit close together and squeeze each other's hands while our bellies were expanding with unreleased giggles. There is nothing worse than a fit of giggles in the middle of an awkward situation and an awkward situation is exactly what you can insert here. We all sat in her small living room while the muted television flashed images of some old western I only caught up on when we visited every few months. We sat there in the silence passing looks around while the husband and wife tried to fill the space with the kinds of questions designed for catching up. We listened while her husband, dressed in his overalls, told stories that stretched on overlong so that by the time the end came, no one could remember what the beginning had been about. The little girl and I sometimes escaped to another sitting area and away from the adults to let some of our laughter free and then proceeded to make up stories about all the glass objects collecting dust around the house. It wasn't a bad situation, it was just uncomfortable. But I will tell you a secret: contained inside the atmosphere of that house, charged with silent discomfort, I felt profoundly equal. An equal recipient of the awkwardness, an equal recipient of the Christmas presents that did not at times make sense, an equal recipient of trying to find a less dirty corner to sit in, an equal recipient of sitting in a room saying things while saying absolutely nothing at all. Inside that house it was hard for the body to relax because of the dirt and the dust that was turning the blue dress on the china doll a murky purple, but maybe in that house was also the place in Alabama that I felt the most equal.

The husband's step mom, while alive, was my favorite. She was frail for as long as I knew her and soft spoken. I understand that my experience of her may have been different than what he had grown up with, but in my time with her, I always felt she saw me. Saw me beyond flesh and skin and into something beyond that. Soul and spirit, maybe? It wasn't her words that left me feeling that way but something about her presence. Something about her invited a sort of softening, allowing a momentary feeling of peace to settle. I did not feel confused about whether I was wanted or allowed when I sat beside her while she rocked in her reclining chair. I noticed the efforts she made to indoctrinate me into the rituals held dear by the other children, like the way she offered us golden Oreos as soon as our feet made it to the kitchen. I felt welcomed by her to the best of her ability and I felt like she was proud of me. Not because of charity or because I had come out of a bad situation. Just proud of me full stop. When she passed away a few years later, I felt the loss profoundly. The husband's dad was never unkind but I experienced him as emotionally detached and maybe being around him made some sense in my mind about the husband's behaviors and shape shifting moods. There was a lot of silence in that house but this time it felt a little less awkward and a little more peaceful. Like I could settle into my own thoughts for a while even as we sat together in living room. I felt that a lot of affection lived inside that house while the step mom was still living, though no one knew how to turn that affection into conversations about anything beyond the surface. The house felt affectionately neutral, that is how I would describe it. If there were ways I was not treated like the other children, they were easier to miss because the environment was not one that was vibrant with outright and demonstrative favoritism and affection. That was reserved for the wife's family.

The merits of the last house in Alabama, and the one we spent the most time at, would not be difficult for the naked eye to miss. Where the other two homes had been loud with silence, this house seemed always to be bursting with noise and personality. Everyone seemed to be a character, entirely distinct and unique yet with the unifying thread of shared southern ideals. The wife's accent intensified as soon as our feet crossed the threshold of the door and I noticed how the husband's did the same. Inside that house family was second only to God and it was this truth that amplified my experience of longing to belong and the grief of knowing that I was not fully accepted. I felt this house as the one most full of warmth and love and the place where my non equity was the most exemplified. Don't misunderstand me, no one was unkind to me directly. Everyone employed their best southern charm and treated me with warmth and kindness and I do genuinely believe that within the lens that they had made me make sense, there was genuine care. I loved the wife's mother. I loved standing with her in the open kitchen mixing ingredients for banana pudding. She'd set a bowl of just the homemade vanilla pudding to the side for me, adorned with a crown of 'nilla wafers, knowing how much I despised bananas. We made pecan pies and talked about litera- ture and old movies. Everyone treated her so delicately as if she might shatter into a million pieces at any time but I always believed that if anyone would have had the space to confront issues like racism it might have been her. Her mind felt the most malleable or maybe that is what I like to tell myself, I cannot be sure. But I will never know since it was never discussed.

What I am saying is that the ways that I was unequal were not always direct. No one was verbalizing that to me. I participated in the gatherings just like everyone else. But inside that house in small town Alabama, with all the grandkids squeezed around the dining room table or sitting together in the living room, I still had the feeling that I was trespassing. I felt it every time I went to get water out of the refrigerator and saw its stainless steel surface ornamented with the faces of the other children. Even after being called daughter for years, my picture was never there to greet me when I refilled my glass. I asked the wife once, after us three children had recently taken school pictures, why she never even bothered to bring a copy of mine to Alabama. I was asking because my heart was being smothered under the constant reminder that I was daughter but not really. I wanted her to know that it hurt me that she did not bring a picture of me at all. It hurt more than if she had shoved the smooth and glistening surface of my picture into their hands and they had elected not to hang it up. At least then she would have been acknowledging me to them as hers. By handing them three photos instead of two she would be saying something to them about who I was to her. All I ever wanted was a parent who was proud to call me theirs in every way. I do not remember what she said in response to my question but it does not matter because she did nothing differently after that. Her purse was always naked of a photo of me and I never did see my face on the refrigerator in the end.

Alabama seemed only to solidify the bond between the little girl and me. Odd for different reasons, we stood out starkly against the norms of Southern culture and expectations, particularly noticeable with the wife's family. The lines were drawn plainly though without explicit definition. We understood what a girl was supposed to be and act like. We understood from the proper mannerisms and uniform interests and from the curled hair and makeup done just so. The daughter was at times socially awkward and odd in her interests and I was odd because I was black and an outsider that would not normally belong nestled within this particular family within this particular town. Yet though we were partially unified in our oddities, I still felt utterly alone in an experience of separateness that she could not relate to. I felt alone in an experience no one seemed to relate to or seemed to care was happening altogether. Like when both of our birthdays came around in the middle of summer. Year after year I watched the little girl's face light up when a birthday card would arrive in the mail or when the phone rang and it was the grandparents on the other end, or years later when it was a text message illuminating the screen of her own cell phone. I watched as those cards and messages acknowledged the day as unique and special, worth remembering, do you understand me? A few weeks later when my birthday arrived, it was my heart that was left to make meaning of the negative space. My hands were void of cards and my phone was empty of calls or messages though my eyes were longing for the screen to light up and my hands were longing for paper to grip themselves around.

Anything to whisper to me: you are special and worth remembering and mostly, you belong. It felt like such an easy thing for the husband and wife to go to bat for me for but they never did. I don't think it even dawned on them that it might be causing spears of pain to splinter my insides. I could not seem to make the variables add up. Why agree to take me if I would always exist on the outside of some very basic experiences. Why take me if you were not willing to fight for me? Inside I felt like something was withering away. I wanted to ask why no one was reaching out to me from Alabama. I wanted to ask but I was afraid to seem ungrateful. I wanted to ask but even though my heart was broken, I wasn't certain if it was selfish to want more. Is it selfish to want more? Or rather, is it selfish to want the same? I could never be sure. I spent my birthdays at war within myself. One part felt petty for being so impacted while the other was asphyxiating from a cocktail of isolation and longing. It might not make sense to you, but on those days, when my otherness felt so explicit, I wished I could rewind my life and return to that last day at the townhouse. I wished I could go back home to Mum and my sisters where at least there was some form of uniformity of experience, where there was, perhaps, a uniformity in invisibility.

One Christmas, when I was making little clay figurines as a hobby, I made the wife's mother a present that was little figures of all the grandchildren. I made mine last, pondering overlong about whether or not she or they would want the evidence of my existence standing so plainly in their home. I didn't know but I put myself there, on the edge, brown skin and a purple dress. I did it because I did not have the heart not to claim myself as part of something. I did it because I wanted to belong somewhere just as much as the other kids did.

FEATURES

Today, for the first time in a long while I had the strange thought that I missed my mother. It happened while I sat in my dimly lit office sipping my lukewarm coffee. It happened while I furrowed my brow at the overcast sky hanging low over the city. When my eyes worked together to narrow their focus and bring into view my slight reflection looking lazily back at me in the window. That's when the thought wriggled free from the tangles of my subconscious, swam upward and lingered, blurry at first but still there. I closed my eyes to make it out, focused, then shivered at its unfamiliarity.

I miss her, I thought to myself, followed promptly by, how strange it is to exist in the world and never behold the face of the woman that bore you. Another shiver then, how strange, indeed that my friends will never know the face from which I inherited my features. That no one will ever gasp at the eerie resemblance between she and me, nor catch me mid laugh and remark, "you have your mother's laugh," or "you sounded just like her when you said that."

I studied myself a little more - the broad nose flanked by round nostrils that flared without permission when I was irritated; the almond eyes, curved upward at the ends and cloaked in eyelashes that insisted on being a kinky mass, no matter how much mascara I applied; the lips full and downward sloping at the corners.

I sighed, blinked back the misty tears beginning to cloud my vision. Something about seeing myself trapped in that dusty window like some sort of apparition, manifest but not quite, made my throat start to twist itself closed.

I blinked some more.

That's when it dawned on me, as the first tear slipped out of my eye, giving way to one more and then another, that perhaps it was not her that I missed at all, but the sensation of recognizing myself in the face of someone else - the uncanny way a sense of home is crafted in the silent resemblance between a mother and child - the way the twin silhouettes of her nose and mine might say to the world without words, she belongs to me and I belong to her.

Yes, I nodded silently, I miss that.

Suddenly the absence of her felt like the strangest vacancy. As if my features themselves were refugees, standing at the uneven border of the great void separating them from home, yet twitching at the knowledge that home would not be the sanctuary they longed so desperately for, even if they could make it back there.

I could feel the sturdy hand of grief pulling me downward into myself.

I have learned not to fight it when it comes.

It is a dreadful waste of energy in the end, to fight against it.

"Where do we go from here?" the features shouted into the void.

But the void returned no sound.

In Alabama, and also when Alabama came to visit us in Atlanta, I was a scholar learning about the place the wife had learned to keep the peace over anything. Her ability to be silent or good natured was indeed a marvel. I understood it as an unspoken family rule but it did not mean I was immune to the pain of her passivity, because that commitment to keeping the peace left me standing there, alien already, and further unprotected. In addition to missed birthdays and absent school photos, I was left alone to contend with the wife's family's beliefs about race and about people with skin like mine.

Once when Alabama came to Atlanta for a visit, we all sat around the television watching the new Karate Kid movie. The air was still and seemingly unthreatening while we laughed in unison at the antics of the actors on the screen. Somewhere in between commentaries about the differences between the original film and this one, the little girl chimed in and started swooning about how cute she thought Jaden Smith was. I laughed along with her and agreed wholeheartedly since I had been thinking something similar.

And then the little cousin from Alabama, under two years younger than the little girl, making her 9 or 10 at the time, chimed in,

"Ewww," she said.

The sister and I looked at each other in confusion. I was blinking and trying to reorient myself in case I had disappeared to the nameless place and missed something. As if to clear things up she finished,

"It's disgusting to think someone of a different race than you is cute."

I felt like someone had used their right fist across my face and their foot against my belly. For a few seconds my heart was living inside my throat. I looked around, tracing the faces of every adult seated in the space, expecting, or hoping rather, to see outrage living in the lines of their faces. Surely. Surely, my insides were shrieking. But there was nothing, not even a whisper of distress. The room felt still as if nothing out of the ordinary had been said while inside I was having something very adjacent to a crisis. My eyes landed finally on the wife's face. Looking and looking and waiting while she avoided making eye contact with me. The seconds were passing by and her mouth did not stretch open. She said nothing. She said nothing while I, her self proclaimed daughter, sat in a room of people who thought it was disgusting to be attracted to someone with skin like mine. It felt like everything before that moment was the familiar sound a shoe makes, at first a whistle when flying backward, as if in warning, and her silence, the sharp crack that follows when shoe connects with skin and causes the ripple.

I stood up and walked into the kitchen. I was equal portions rage, heartbreak and helplessness. She followed me, calling out my name as if asking my feet to stop moving. I turned to face her.

"They don't have anything against *you*, sweetie," she said.

As if being the exception to their hatred would somehow make me feel any better or safer. I looked at her. I kept my face a stone even though her excuse for them was causing my heart to hemorrhage. I just kept looking while all the feelings were passing through me in tremors yet the tears would not fall. I felt naked. I felt naked like that day in the mirror when Mum was twisting my nipples and relating the form of my body to that of an animal. I looked at her because she was letting them do the same with their words. I gave her my back and walked to my bedroom and she let me. She let me walk away all alone again to manage the internal bleeding.

REST

Where do you find rest
    When the protectors are the perpetrators

My best friend calls - we weep
    "what will we tell your boys about the police?" I whisper
    One son favors the father -
    his skin shades lighter than his brother, who favors the mother
    My sister, my friend
    To fill the space between her shortness of breath,
    "what will we tell them about power?"

I can't breathe, she moans
    Me either

I roll over and go to sleep
    I sleep in black
    I dream in black
    I wake Black

I weep

Where do you find rest
    When guns aren't the only form of weapons
    When excuses are a knee against your neck
    When neutrality tears your flesh
    When the silence hums like the flaming metal of a bullet
    Passing through sacred air
    Leaving you still and
    Naked of breath—

I can't breathe

Where do you find rest

When rest itself feels like a privilege
When peace feels intangible
When your body tingles with the familiarity —
Of the protectors being the perpetrators
All over again

Where do you find rest?

I felt their racism long before then. I understood that the only reason I had a seat at the Thanksgiving table and presents under the Christmas tree is because they could justify my presence as an act of charity. At times over dinners, the wife's brother would parrot off stories about the kids at the school he taught at. There was a particular flavor to the stories when the children were black. He'd tell the stories about their impulsivity and disrespect in a way that made them criminal or barbaric. As if their behavior confirmed the twisted narrative about what it meant to have brown skin. Then he would look at me enthusiastically while nodding his head,

"Right?" he'd say and wait for me to agree.

I looked around the room. I looked one by one at the faces gathered around the table. I let my eyes linger longer on the face of one of the cousins. I had always thought of him as wildly impulsive and disrespectful. He was just like the boys in the story except he was white so his behavior did not make him criminally flawed. It just made him a naughty teenager. One by one my eyes traveled in a circle. I could feel the wife's brothers eyes still on me and waiting for my affirmative. In that moment I felt both that there was no one like me at that table and also truly, there was no one for me at that table either. There in the slow motion silence I felt both the the weight of invisibility and of visibility at once. I want to say that the lips did not part and say back,

"Right."

I hope with everything in me that I did not reject myself so entirely that I affirmed him. But I cannot be sure.

Later when I would try to talk to the wife about it in private, when I tried to paint for her a picture of the danger and loneliness of those moments, she would simply say,

"Well you aren't *that* kind of black."

I felt an internal fracture then. One part relief to have some distance from whatever kind of black might put me in danger inside that house and another part completely devastated. All I wanted was for her to march into the living room of that house and make her voice a drum of warning that boomed,

"You cannot talk about my child that way."

But she never did. She kept her voice on mute and so no one ever did stand up for me.

Late at night I crawled into the bed where I slept when we visited. I turned onto my side and wrapped my arms across my chest. I felt like I might come apart from the grief unless I held myself together. Unless I did not press my hands against my own skin to keep the seams from bursting. I squeezed the eyes shut and asked the tears not to fall but it was useless. I was overfull. Equal portion rage and despair. The rage always came first - violent and hot while it shook the body and the words I wished I'd spoken formed a song inside my mind. I let it have its way with me. Let it wrap its veiny arms around my entirety and have its way with me. Let it roar to life while I shook violently and the sweat coated my silk sleeping bonnet. I let my hands turn into fists while I held inside them the awareness that while I lay there in the sleepless grips of despair, the rest of the house was sleeping peacefully. Can someone please explain to me why the perpetrators always seem to slumber so easily? It hardly seems fair.

I wanted to stay there. I wanted to stay in the heated power of my own rage. But the rage, like a fever, always breaks. Then the slow descent into pain. That is what you would see here, the violent breaking of rage's fever that invites the shift into the soul's tearful shudders. As the mind plays the night's events one more time but in slow motion. Inside that mind movie the actions of the extended family and inactions of the husband and wife manifested like hangers and wooden spoons in their hands. Flying backward in unison, and connecting just the same. In truth I would have preferred abuse against the body. I would have preferred physical scars and bruises to how meaningless their inactions made me feel and to the awareness of how utterly unworthy I must be if in the face of danger they would choose silence over protecting me.

A few years later, one of the cousins was dating a boy who was half black. It was a shock to me since it was the same cousin who had, years before, proclaimed attraction to a different race as disgusting. I felt proud of her evolution but her mother, the wife's sister, was in uproar about the entire thing and he was not allowed to come to Thanksgiving. I asked the wife, already knowing the answer, if he was a bad kid or if he was a trouble maker, or maybe he was disrespectful. I was listing the questions out of pure desperation, hoping for what was true to not be true. Yet her answer to every question posed was no. The reason he could not come to thanksgiving was because he was black.

I looked at the wife directly in the eyes. I let the silence between us lengthen into something uncomfortable. I kept my eyes looking right into hers as in the silence I offered her one more chance to stretch her jaws open and say something. Please, the silence was imploring:

PLEASE CHOOSE me
    please see me
    please fight for me
    please unmute your voice and protect me
    please tell me I am worthy of these things
    PLEASE

BUT THE WORDS NEVER CAME. They never came.

I DID NOT GO BACK to Alabama after that. It was because I was tired of begging to be fought for and it was because I decided that I would start fighting for myself instead. By this time I had been a spectator to the ways that the wife was willing to stand up for her own children inside that house in Alabama. Though they too had to claw and beg for her to do it, eventually she did do it for them. Do you know how it feels to continuously be reminded that it is not that someone is incapable of fighting, it is just that they do not see you as worth fighting for? Do you know how it eats away at your sense of worthiness, how you just begin to feel less than human? Or maybe not even human at all. It is its own form of torture.

I find it hard to write about this. The grief sprouts anew inside my body every time a word manifests on this paper. The grief and something with it. Shame. I am still dealing with the shame that I myself was silent for so long. That I did not stretch my own jaws open in defense of myself and of people like me. That I did not stand up and redignify myself. I feel in those moments I failed to make my daddy proud. My daddy who always taught me to champion my brown skin and who was brave in the face of so much adversity and used his voice to fight for what was right. I wish he had been there. All those years I wished he had been there. He would have gripped his hands onto either one of my shoulders and shaken me gently. Shaken me until I came back to myself and until I remembered not to sacrifice any piece of myself to make other people more comfortable. He would have reminded me that their discomfort was not mine to manage. But he was not there and so in those moments I was silent too. I am not proud of it, but I didn't know what to do. What would you have done if you were me? I felt so alone inside a world with such disdain for people with my skin, yet reliant on them for food and shelter and a sense of family that I didn't know what to do. I am not proud of the complications that arose in my own perception of my own blackness. How for so long I too grew tired and at times loathsome of my own identity. I didn't know how to hold my blackness proudly when being black itself seemed to keep me on the fringes of love, acceptance and safety. I won't lie to you — I have fought against myself for a long time. It is a shame really. To have been raised at the start of my life with my blackness so integrated into my identity to then immigrate into a world and family that made my skin feel heavy, like a cloak, criminal and ladened with shame. It has taken time to claim myself in all the ways others failed to claim me and to fiercely re-integrate a part of me that was so viciously ostracized. I am only telling you this because that is the deal we have made, when you first started reading this story. I have promised to tell you the truth.

Years later, after George Floyd was murdered on the street in broad daylight, and after I had come to learn what it meant to be loved in my entirety, then the husband told me on the phone that he had talked to a black friend of his from high school about race and racism. He had told his friend he had a black daughter. The friend told him he had no idea. That in all the pictures the husband had posted on facebook in all these years, fifteen years since I first moved into their house, the friend would never have known that there was a black girl living in his house. A black girl the husband was now calling "daughter." He was saying the words to me as if telling someone about the weather casually. I maintained my composure. Kept the grief back though I could feel it bubbling inside my stomach and trying to shiver its way up and up and up. I maintained my composure and had the discussion with him. If he was looking for absolution and for comfort as he always did, I did not offer him any. I wanted the words he was saying to plant themselves inside of his body, take root and grow into something uncomfortable that would perhaps invite him to change. Inside I felt devastated. I felt enraged and grief stricken. It was the validation coming out of his lips inadvertently as he told the story that was making my body feel suddenly too small to house all the emotions living inside of it. I got off the phone. I threw it against the wall to relieve some of the tension vibrating under my skin. I called a friend and wailed into the phone, gulping and gasping and fighting for air, while my throat felt it was narrowing to the size of a straw. All at once I felt validated in the feelings that my blackness, among other things, had been a thing that kept me from being fully welcomed. All at once I felt how I had been in the house but not a member of a home. All at once I felt all the years of being unprotected and unclaimed. All the years of being there but not there at all. The ways I was, perhaps, useful to the them, but never one of them. I felt like a commodity; unclothed entirely of my humanity. Do you know what it is like to hear someone parrot to you that they never had the courage, or love, to post you proudly on their facebook page? I felt his wrists gripping onto me as he claimed, only now, to have a "black daughter." Now that his proximity to me and to my blackness might save his image out in the world. I wanted to peel his hands off of me. Finger by scrawny finger, remove any stake he believed to have on me. Remind him that when I needed to be a daughter he had instead stripped me of any right to need, to speak, to be anything other than grateful. I wanted to remind him that when my blackness had been targeted his mouth had remained clamped shut and that he had said nothing in defense of me or people who looked like me. I wanted him to know that he could not claim me now and only for his own benefit. It was all coming back to me in flashbacks, image after image and moment after moment of feeling like by existing I was taking something from someone. How he had opened his mouth only to belittle me aggressively and kept it clamped shut while leaving my personhood under attack. I felt like the grief might rise up and kill me.

"How can you treat someone like that?" I whispered to my friend once the worst of the sobs had eased and the memories had slowed to a trickle. Once my throat unclenched to allow more air to enter my body.

Later on I found a picture of myself as a teenager and taped it to my refrigerator. I wanted to offer that child a piece of the dignity that was so viciously denied her. To put her on the fridge and offer her visibility and pride of place somewhere. A home inside my home. I looked into her eyes while the tears were dripping onto the floor.

"I love you. And I'm proud of you," I said to her round face and to her brown skin and finally I meant it. Seeing the picture taped on the fridge made the waves of grief unleash anew.

"How could you not love her?" I was screaming out into my empty apartment as I laid crumpled on the floor and, "She's so beautiful."

I texted the picture to the friend who'd stayed on the line while I wept.

"Here she is," I typed.

"I love her so much," she wrote back.

"Me too," I replied.

GEORGE

At night I dreamed I found myself evicted from my slumbering body
    Floating, an apparition - in motion
    through time
    through space
    I stretched myself into the lifeless cavity of his body
    Flexed my phantom fingers to fill the spaces of his hands
    like a latex glove
    The throbbing of my heart reviving him - for a moment
    I felt the the cool concrete crushing against my left cheek
    I heard the chorus of bystanders pleading
    I saw the tears dripping onto the pavement
    Drip.
    In the moments before
    Drip.
    Asphyxiation

At night I dreamed I found myself evicted from my slumbering body
    Fitted neatly inside his silhouette of flesh
    A moment of temporary inception - intersection
    I in him and he in me
    Body dead, Spirit undead
    A collision of souls
    He tilted his phantom head to fill the expanse of my mind, snug
    like a baseball cap
    And stretched my awareness out into a projector screen
    He saw the police escort terrorists delicately down the Capitol
stairs
    He saw them pause for a photograph
    He saw them never reach for their holsters
    He saw them never press their knees against necks
    He saw them scatter away in fear
    He saw them
    He saw

His hollow eyes whispered across to me
It's not fair
Sunken
It's not fair
Stricken
It's not fair

Fearful I might split us both in two
From wielding the force of his grief and terror
The twin weight of my very own
Confusion and rage
I bowed my head to sever the connection

At night I dreamed I found myself evicted from my slumbering body
Floating, an apparition - in motion
through time, floating,
through space
Until once again tethered to the familiarity of my own physical
being
And upon waking
It's not fair
Wilting
It's not fair
Wailing
It's not fair
Weeping

It's not fair

BIRTHRIGHT

Special — Unique — Visible
How do you reclaim those words when
they feel impregnated with affliction
Robust and bellies full
of the memorialized [and ongoing]
reverberations of trauma
with the echoes of innocence torn asunder

When visibility has been a noose around your neck
When visibility has been assault
When visibility has been the companion of violation

How do you reclaim those words when
the fear has simply metamorphosed
from the anticipation of your body being colonized
Uninvited hands welcoming themselves into
and against sacred places
Exploration without permission
To the anticipation of a no knock
police imposed execution

When visibility has been death

Inside my head, Hope cartwheels against an invisible landscape:
being free is your birthright, she chants
While her palms nurse violation's lacerations
Special and free
While her song tills the latent soil of timid dreams
Unique and free
While her tears stoke the dried embers of empowerment
Visible and free

How do you reclaim those words when

How do **You reclaim those words when**
You reclaim those words when
You **Reclaim those words**
Breathe, laugh, soar, dream
Remember
Being free is your birthright

PART III

As I was writing the first words of this story, I wondered what I would tell you in the end. What final words would leak out of my fingertips as we glanced back together, our arms perhaps on each other's shoulders in solidarity. I wondered what I would say as the elongated fingers of night unclasped from around me, that full moon's slight nod of the head, a sacred permission to step over the threshold and into something new. A new way of being. I wondered if you'd feel my chest cavity expanding with gratitude, my breath sailing out like a song into the night, my greatest teacher. I feel a certain kind of pressure here. Maybe you are feeling it too. It is telling me to manifest a silky piece of colored ribbon and tie this up into something tidy. To find a way to make a meaning out of all the words that are scattered amongst these pages.

I have always imagined this book in three parts, each one saying something about my experience of family. It is vulnerable to say it but for so long the only way I could imagine this ending was with one more shot at family, a redemptive experience that proved to me and the other people on these pages that I am worthy of a safe experience of family. I do not like the nakedness of typing those words and yet it is the most honest thing I can say here. I did not know how to envision my own sense of worthiness naked of a new external experience, do you understand what I am saying? I could not imagine a way to dignify myself without the approval of others. I had imagined inviting you here into a life and world with my own partner and my own babies running around freely and their existence is what would say to me, and maybe you as well, see girl you are allowed to have a family and with a sigh I would finally be able to release the ache and settle the lies inherited from my first familial experiences. It is the way I had been moving through the world for so long. I'd been glancing into the faces of every person I formed attachments with and interpreting what I saw there as a confirmation or denial of the messages that were still swimming around inside of me. Only it didn't matter how many denials there were because they never did seem to touch the place that was aching. They never could reclothe the girl standing naked in front of a wall of mirrors or soothe the little baby crouched on the floor with shards of glass in her hair. They could never help the teenage girl recognize her brown skin with pride instead of seeing it as a burden and obstacle to receiving a belonging she was desperate for. The denials could not reach them because I was not connected to them myself. I was complicit in forgetting these pieces of me that had always longed to be seen and further, I did not actually believe anything different about them than what had been spoken over them. It was a brutal realization, to notice that I could not take in something from others that I was unable to offer to myself or believed myself to be worthy of. And yet that realization itself propelled me into a different kind of journey than I originally anticipated. A journey of self confirmation and of self belonging. A homecoming, perhaps.

I have not written these words because I have a trope to offer to you. I do not have a silky ribbon or any platitudes that will make what has been brutal less so. I have written these words to memorialize both the pain and the power of remembering. For so long I have been a hostage to the forgetting. I forgot in order to stay alive and yet the forgetting itself became a new kind of death. A death disguised as fragmentation, because by forgetting the experience I was forgetting myself as well. I am not saying I am defined by the things that were done and left undone, and yet I cannot reject or forget the experiences without also rejecting myself. It is because an iteration of me was there during each of these moments and she is worth remembering and seeing, don't you agree? Perhaps I am me because of what has transpired and perhaps I am me in spite of what has transpired as well. Maybe it is through the remembering that we begin to integrate and through the integrating that we can begin to reclaim.

MAMA

I carried your body with me
    Hung you like my favorite outer garment on the hook by the door
    Wound myself in you before my feet crossed the threshold
    I wanted to pretend you were a cocoon,
    a coat composed of long strands of silk wound tightly around
my core
    I wanted to pretend you were a dark hole,
    a bunker shielding me from the world, or the world from me,
    I could not ever be sure
    I wanted to pretend that your intentions were pure,
    imagine you to be the arms from which
    I would eventually take off in wondrous flight
    And though my wings never seemed to reach formation,
    I did not blame you,
    believing that the fault was with me.

I carried your blood with me
    Out there the wind swished around my body,
    as if to say, "girl, you were meant to soar. To shine.
    To be —free"
    But inside, you wound your silky threads into my ears
    and shushed those wispy wind whispers, saying
    "the wind does not know you as I do,"
    and wound yourself ever more tightly
    around my aching frame and
    I trusted you,
    trusted this blood bond confinement,
    although unsure if the pain would ever truly be
    the inception of freedom

I carried your words with me
    like a diction induced migraine behind my left eye
    On repeat, mumbles, shouts — until—

once, in the secret of night
The whispers of the wind creeped in on tiptoes
and conjured up images behind my eyelids
and inside those dreams
you were, astonishingly,
embodied as a coarsely stitched straitjacket
and not as the cocoon I had always imagined you to be
And though I tried,
[And I did try, mama]
I could not unsee what I had,
while sleeping, seen.
And in the light of morningtide
the long strands of you felt like
a silken home no longer

Mama,

This is the act of unzipping myself from you
    Of sitting with a silver spoon
    and scrapping you out from the marrow of my bones
    This is the act of resurrection and regeneration
    of choosing me instead of the impeding comfort of you
    I hope you can forgive me
    This act of emancipation will, perhaps, feel
    like betrayal
    like disownment
    like abandonment
    will, certainly, feel
    selfish
    And it is—
    I cannot fly with the weight of you
    pressed against my back
    But—

I will carry your spirit with me

like a pin pressed into the tips of my just sprouted wings,
that beautiful, untouched, essence of who you are
and who you have yet to be
And as I begin to catch speed,
To soar, as I have always dreamed,
I hope to pass you in the height of flight
Your broad wings singing the song of emancipation
Your own liberation from the apparitions of your past
There is room in the sky for both of us
I hope you'll meet me there
Someday

I was not the initiator of this remembering. It initiated itself and I am grateful because I cannot say with honesty that I would have chosen it. I was under the impression that I had successfully overcome my own experience and that I was doing just fine. In some ways I was. I had done everything I had set my mind to. I had made it to college. I was in Graduate school and on my way to building a career I could be proud of. I had trouble feeling close to people but many people felt close to me, and that felt adequate enough. I had mastered the character of composure so well that I myself was a daytime believer. What I am saying is that I was living and so I was failing to register the fact that I was not alive. I was failing to register how the fear still had me so firmly in it's grips and how I was still letting it drive me with such a singular focus that I was forgetting about the parts that were left starving and alone in the other place, though it was I who had promised to return to them.

"Keep going," I was telling myself - believing, and indeed hoping, that if I could just work hard enough, be financially secure enough, find a place to live on my own, *then* I would finally feel safe. I was still feeling the imminence of danger like a knife pressed against my throat. Though in the day I was the poster child for resilience, it was when the sky turned black and I laid in bed and while looking around my apartment, tried every night to coach the body into believing that it was safe to sleep. Still the body could not, when my eyelids fluttered shut, submit to the vulnerability and defenselessness of rest, even after I was finally living alone. The fear came in the night as an unwelcome movie in my mind, or like leaden sensation pressed against my chest. I was still running and running and running. Even while sleeping I was still running and then waking with a start. Repeat. I attributed the inability to rest to a lack of physical safety and security and so instead of stopping to tend to what was really fueling the cycle, I just worked harder and ran faster. That is why I am saying that I am grateful the remembering initiated itself. I am not sure I would have ever chosen it. I am stubborn, as you have learned by now.

It started one morning while I was sitting at a training during my Graduate studies. The disintegration did perhaps precede this exact moment. Being in graduate school to become a therapist requires a sort of emotional undressing and so maybe I was already beginning to come apart in ways I had been avoiding. The speaker had the type of voice that invited my edges to further soften. It was soupy with warmth and what I can only describe as paternal. He was moving around the front of the room and he was saying that we weren't created to calm ourselves down. The statement was simple enough but I could feel the way it was suddenly causing something in me to start stirring around nervously. I tapped my foot quickly on the ground, my well developed cheat code to do exactly what he was saying we weren't created to do: calm myself down. I was telling myself I was not there to feel. I was there to learn so I tapped my foot and chewed on my cuticles to ground myself. Later he handed out a questionnaire that we could use in our assessment with clients. I had many papers stacked in front of me by then and so I accepted this one without concern. My eyes scanned the questions one by one. The paper was full of questions but the word *comfort* was popping off the page as if typed out in red ink. Seeing it there in front of me over and over again was making my body start to quiver. Comfort. Just that one word holding hands with others and the edges began to vibrate away. My eyes kept moving against the questions. One by one while the room and everything else started to fade into the background. One by one while my eyes became so full of tears that one blink would tip them over. He was still speaking at the front of the room but I could not make out what he was saying though I was straining to hold onto his words. To keep me in the room so that the emotions did not take me elsewhere. I was closing my eyes and asking the ears to turn his sounds into words but all I could hear was how the breath was moving in and out of my body shakily. The remembering had come. I would not have called it that at the time. At the time I sat there in a vortex of something that felt at once forceful and at once incredibly gentle. I excused myself quickly to the bathroom. I sat in the stall while the tears were falling. I sat there and had the feeling like the stall was not big enough to contain all the pieces of me that were suddenly present. They were all there, pushing against the walls of the flimsy grey stall and with sallow eyes that were asking me, wordlessly, about comfort. I felt I had no answer to offer them. How could I offer them what had never been offered to me?

I sat in that stall while I pressed my face into my hands. I let my palms make a cup for my tears while the air entered my body in shudders. I suddenly felt so tired. As if my body was registering almost three decades of sleepless nights in that one instant. The remembering had come and I could feel the choice plainly like someone had scribbled it illicitly onto the stall walls in black sharpie: keep running or slow down.

I'M afraid something will happen to me if I don't
    keep moving
    If my chest isn't heaving and my legs aren't aching at
    the force of constant exertion
    If I'm not out of breath and exhausted—
    am I safe?

MY INSIDES FELT SHREDDED, like everything was struggling against itself. I felt a little bit like I was choosing between death and death, terrified that if I submitted to what was happening and went in search of myself, I might find that everything that was said about me had been true. What if I saw myself and I discovered that I really was unworthy, ungrateful, unlovable. What if it was true that I was not worth being visible, displayed with pride against a stainless steel refrigerator? What if it was all true? I didn't think I could face it. I was afraid it might kill me to face it. And yet comfort kept bouncing around inside my head, bumping against every fear like in a game of pinball.

COMFORT. Comfort. Comfort.

· · ·

IN THE END I sighed loudly and collected myself. The submission was not gentle but would have sounded more like,

"FINE!" if I had spoken it out loud.

I was tired of fighting. I was just so tired. I typed out a shaky text to a friend asking for a referral for a therapist. I told her I needed someone who could be a beacon and a force. Someone to hold the edges while I came apart and someone who would not break underneath the storm I felt was coming.

JOURNAL ENTRY

What should I call this place that both feels too fast and
    also achingly slow—this place that insists
    on holding me hostage in the tension between
    — old and new —
    A forced self observation that is demanding me to
    untangle myself — to let what has felt
    securely fastened to my sense of self
    fall away
    hopefully making way for a rebirth that invites
    a deeper sense of congruence

Perhaps life has taught me that I am meant to crawl -
    belly against rough earth,
    inch by brutal inch, when really
    I have always been destined to fly

What does it take to grow wings— ?

I always imagined the metamorphosis to be
    the easiest bit but this erosion of myself
    — this chaotic melting —
    the dissolving of what no longer serves me
    yet retaining what is necessary, it feels like
    near death

Perhaps it is the vague awareness of wings developing
    from all that is being sloughed away
    that is keeping me going
    Or perhaps it is the knowing that
    transforming is no longer a choice
    the old center cannot hold

But here:

— inside the painful middle —
it feels quite simply like choosing between near death
and near death
the old place will kill me
but this middle place could do the same
this place between old form and new wings
Sigh—
There are days I wish I could return to being
numbly contented in what was once
enough, but

I can't unsee the possibility of a life with wings

And so I am trying to teach myself to relax into
    this painful disintegration, trusting,
    or attempting to,
    that the melting is not death
    but rebirth

I n my first session, I was giving the therapist a summary of what had transpired in my lifetime. It wasn't difficult. Back then I could still tell the story without a crumb of emotion entering my voice.

"Do you do that a lot?" she asked me in a short stretch of silence.

I looked at her blankly. I kept looking at her while blinking and trying to remember what I had just been saying. Nothing was coming to mind and so I had no clue what she was asking me about. I could feel a vague annoyance living inside my arched eyebrows.

"Do what?" I said back.

That was when she made her words a mirror and held it in my face so I could see my own reflection. She did so by reciting the last moments back to me and making me aware of the way my eyes had looked up and to my right and I had just seemed to disappear from the room. It was, of course, a trip to the nameless place that she was describing. She had watched me become a split screen right there in front of her. My brain was still there with her, saying the words and answering the questions, yet my heart had gone elsewhere. There is a strange sort of intimacy in being so seen, I won't lie to you. With warmth in her eyes she was seeing me better than I could see myself. I could not refute what she had said back to me and yet I wanted her to take the words out of our shared ecosystem and put them back inside her body immediately. It was because as she said the words, she was also inviting my heart to come back into the room, and with my heart the raw emotion that belonged to the words I was saying. Her softness was inviting a softening in me.

That is how it went for a long time. Bit by bit I plugged the emotion back in and bit by bit I felt it all. I let all of it come alive. Bit by bit I grieved and offered comfort. Grieved and offered comfort. Over and over again. I remembered and by remembering, I held hands with every single piece of me and bore witness to their pain and after bearing witness worked to integrate them into my life and by doing so reconstruct a sense of wholeness that had previously been obliterated. Let me tell you something please: I had not been far off when, in that bathroom stall, I had feared the coming alive might at times resemble dying. There were times I felt like an exposed nerve ending walking around my life and times I became exasperated. I wanted to tell my therapist that she had broken me and to please reinstate my ability to completely disconnect immediately. There were times I thought I had felt it all only to find a new place that needed tending and it was in those moments that I wondered if this was all worth it. At times I missed the compartmentalization because I was afraid I could not possibly hold myself together and stay alive. It felt a little like giving birth to myself over and over again and instead of turning away in disgust, instead of rejecting what came forth, which would have been all too familiar, continuing to look and to hold until I myself softened. Until my gaze softened and I could see the self standing there, separate from the lies that had been branded into her skin. And then hold my arms out in a circle and offer a place. That is what it took to learn to love myself differently than I had ever been loved and to tentatively begin letting others love me in kind. That is what it took to learn that the actions and inactions of the parents in my lifetime were not a reflection of me. They did not mean I was too much or not enough. They did not mean I was unlovable or unworthy. They did not mean I was not worth fighting for. It was not easy to undo the messages I had believed about myself for so long. I felt I had had two chances at family and in both situations there had been rejection and abuse of power. In both situations I had felt like an inconvenience instead of a child. In both situations I had felt disposable and that I was something to be ashamed of. So you understand why it was difficult not to add up the sum of those variables and come to the conclusion that it must be me. That there must simply be something wrong with me. For so long it was the only answer that made sense.

There were times I grew weary of what it took to come alive to myself and there are still times that I am weary with it, but truthfully? I would do it again. To learn to be family to myself and to have all of me I would do it all again. I would fight to have myself all over again and still do because it is the way I rebuild a new narrative. One in which no piece of me is disposable. Maybe not every demolition is permanent destruction. Maybe sometimes we must tear down in order to rebuild.

SOUP

And the skin of my self imposed chrysalis
    strained as the soupy remnants of old form solidified into some-
thing new
    And with it the realization that I will no longer allow myself
    to emerge to crawl green against green leaves
    Hidden and out of view

No—

I will instead accept the gift of a pair of water colored wings
    Relinquish this contract of invisibility that has been my safe haven
    Set my sights on a purpose that is all mine
    Set my sights on more than just living
    Set my sights on being alive

Most of the time the rebuilding felt like re-entering rooms within myself that were freezing and painted with dust and cobwebs. It was a little bit like sitting in the middle of those rooms and letting myself feel the discomfort of being there again. Some rooms were harder to enter than others, and indeed some rooms I had never admitted existed. I had to enter those places first and did so within the incubator of my therapy experience. One by one and upon finding the iteration of myself who was there, learning to be beside her. To let her be little and fall apart for as long as necessary. Stay until our eyes would meet and as she looked up at me, let her see something new reflected back to her. Acceptance, love, belonging. Room by room just like that. First just me and then slowly and tentatively learning to invite others into those places too. And by doing so, letting myself learn something new about being seen and being held by others. There was part of me that wanted to hermit away until I was presentable. I wanted to hide until I was pristine but the hiding kept it all fueling. It kept me believing that in order to have companionship I needed to be strong. It kept me believing that if anyone really came close they would either hurt me or they would not want to stay. It was part of the reconstruction: learning how to let people into the mess while it was still a mess. Learning not to disappear into the pain. Learning not to feign stability and instead send a signal out and trust that my people would come, as I would for them. Come and not cause destruction. Come and not reject. And they did come. They came and they taught me something else about what it means to have family.

I was with a friend once. She was sitting across from me while I did an intensive session. I was laying on the couch across from her and my insides were crumbling. The pain was making my whole body shake violently. That day the work was being with the teenage self. It was validating her experience after she lived alone in a world where no one did so. It was letting her have words instead of imposing words upon her. I did not want to do it at first. I did not want to let myself melt for us. I was gripping some metaphorical guard rails until my palms stung from the tension. I did not want to forget her but I was not sure I could survive the alternative. If I felt what was living inside her body all those years when she herself had contemplated reaching toward death, would it kill me? I could not be sure. In the moments before choosing whether to forget or remember, whether to melt or remain rigid, I was again a split screen embodied. A tug of war within myself.

"I can't feel this," I was saying, "but I can't leave her."

It occurred to me then that maybe I had been parented by people who were resistant to the melting. I did not blame them. The melting is hard work. The remembering is at first registered as a threat to the system, so I understand. But I did wonder what it might have been like had I been parented by people who had melted in order to embrace the entirety of themselves and by embracing themselves perhaps becoming better able to embrace all of me?

With one more staggered breath, I let my fingers relax their hold on the guardrails. I let myself lean all the way in until I was with the teenage pain. I did it because I wanted to offer myself something different this time. I let myself weather the initial rage overtaking my body, rode it high until the rage itself relaxed into a hurt and grief stretching out in every direction and as far as I could see. I knew I could not feel it all myself. I knew my friend was there watching me. Keeping watch as I had asked her to do. Then *comfort* was there again, rising unbidden against the internal chaos. I could feel the need making a pool inside my belly but I was afraid to ask. To now reach beyond offering comfort to myself and instead receive comfort. I had never said the words before and so it was a little bit like learning a brand new language. I opened one eye. I saw her looking at me with tears inside her eyes to match mine. I closed my eye. I breathed to let my esophagus stretch open. Opened both eyes and with a whisper I said,

"Can you rub my back?"

She would have come sooner than when I had asked. I know it because I know her. She had waited because she knew how touch frightened me. And particularly touch when I did not feel in control or when I was falling apart. She knew and so she waited and the waiting allowed me the space to settle the fear and the part of me that was screaming: remember when you promised you'd never let yourself be touched unless you were strong?

"Can you rub my back?" I said and for the first time in my life I did not stifle the whimper. I was thirty two years old and this time I did not stifle the whimper because it deserved to be heard. It had always deserved to be heard.

She rubbed my back while I closed my eyes and wept. While my nose was a faucet and the snot was pouring out thickly. While the caged whimpers were unloosed. Still she kept rubbing my back and stroking my hair. Moving her hand gently across my face. It was difficult to let myself be loved with such tenderness. I kept opening my eyes to look at her. I kept opening my eyes because I was afraid of this moment though I was starving for it as well. I opened my eyes and watched her to make sure she did not shift into something dangerous while she had me lying there, vulnerable and disarmed. I opened my eyes to make sure I was not too much to hold. I opened my eyes to make sure she still wanted to be my friend even though I could not always be strong. I opened my eyes to make sure I should not be taking care of her instead.

"Do you need to go to the bathroom? Do you need to eat? Are you thirsty?" I was asking her.

What I was really saying is, "is this okay?"

And it was. After all this time, it really was okay. With one last sigh, my body finally relaxed into the bliss of being held.

And so maybe too, we have to remember in order to relearn.

REMEMBERING

release me from the brown sludge
    unloose my hands and unchain my feet
    let me build myself a new birth canal and re-emerge
    equal parts safety
    equal parts power
    one hundred percent free
    unleash me and let me roam
    unencumbered and freely
    guarded by a canopy of swaying trees —
    vibrant green
    let me sit overlong in overgrown meadows
    while I watch one single bud endlessly
    while I marvel at its tenderness to the touch
    yet mighty to multiply
    and cover the earth with unrestrained beauty
    all i want is to start again —
    all the way in the beginning when i was safety
    and power slow dancing together
    underneath a bright full moon
    mothered by nature herself and a student to her splendor
    all i want is the space to wonder and lose myself
    in the magnificence of my own imagination
    I remember what it was like then
    to walk bare chested through the grass
    while the uncut blades licked my belly and my knees
    as my face pressed near — nearer still
    to examine the opulent and translucent wings
    of an untamed luna moth
    making a dance floor out of an opening wildflower
    i remember how i giggled with delight
    before the developed instinct to hurry or hide
    or crane my neck to look in terror over
    the dome of my shoulder blade

i remember then the pure magic of myself
immaculate in my unrestraint
wildness embodied
delicateness exemplified
i remember what is was like then
to walk bare chested through the grass
before the pain and before the judgement
before, before, before
when i was invincible and little
strong and achingly tender
safe and powerful
entirely me

As I was writing the first words of this story, I was already wondering what I would tell you at the end. We have stood together in the nighttime of my life. We have trudged through the muddy and dense creeks and clasped our heaving chests up steep mountains. We have lain together on freezing tundra, knees pressed to our chests and wept, tears freezing on our eyelashes. I have stripped myself naked in every word on these pages. I have given my consent to let you leaf through me, let you discover my power and my pride, my softness and my glassy edges. You have witnessed both my humanity and at times, my barbarity. As have I. As your eyes have traveled across these pages, you have been a spectator and participant and I thank you for holding me while I myself was learning what it means to hold myself entirely. In these pages I have not only authored my story but I have authored myself, do you understand me? I have traveled to the nameless place to retrieve all the parts and pieces I ordered to wait behind and stay quiet while I forged a life safe enough for them to emerge into. I have stitched every piece of this story together and by doing so I have stitched myself together so that I am no longer in pieces. So that I can redignify every part of myself and offer them a place in my life and in my world. So that I can look at every iteration of myself and recognize a worthiness inherent to their existence. And by doing so learn to be a safe family first and foremost unto myself. A home — finally. I hope that as you have been a spectator you have also felt a type of invitation to retrieve every piece of yourself and to hold yourself entirely, as you deserve to be held. As we all do.

Before I drift off to sleep, I still find myself uttering my hopes into the blank space. It is a ritual that honors the genesis of this. A ritual that honors a littler version of me who kept hoping and dreaming for something that felt so out of reach. Back then her hopes were simple: all she wanted was to wake up at her own volition. Not to the sound of footsteps moving toward the bedroom door, not to a weight making a dent in her small body, not to the sound of screaming. My breath still stutters as I remember the desperation of those whispers, seeds sown into the ether in hopes that someone was listening. I like to think it was me that was listening. That the grown up version of that baby was listening all along and calling her forward so that we could meet. As we have done across these pages. I close my eyes to feel the fulness of myself stretching out to fill my entire body. I feel the way as I lay inside my bed, I am finally in one piece: mind, body, spirit. That I am a home unto myself. That I am a home unto others. That others are, blessedly, a home unto me. Holding myself this way, holding myself entirely, means the pictures still stretch themselves out inside my mind some nights. It means that the pain still comes and interrupts the steady flow of air as it travels into my body. It means that sometimes the loss feels incredibly overwhelming. It feels important for me to say this here. To say it so that we are on the same page that the remembering, the relearning and the reclaiming do not happen in a straight line. Sometimes they feel like an upward rising and other times they feel like a descent back into grief. Being a home unto myself means a commitment to honoring both. It means celebrating the incredibly vulnerable and playful reclaiming of my littleness while also letting the tears drip down my face for the reasons that the littleness was disrupted to begin with. For me the rising and descent have finally become friends, no longer in competition and instead knowing there is room for them both and enough love to go around. Finally.

A smile spreads slowly across the lips. Across my lips. I inhale and with the sigh of an exhale, sow the seeds of a new dream out into the ether:

LET ME BE THE INTERSECTION OF MY EXPERIENCES. LET ME BE LIGHT AND DARK, BEAUTIFUL AND MARRED, MARKED AND PRISTINE. LET ME BE LOUD AND LITTLE, MIGHTY AND TENDER, LIMPING AND SPRINTING, NEEDED AND NEEDY. FOR SO LONG I HAVE HAD TO CHOOSE TO HOLD MYSELF IN SEGMENTS. FOR SO LONG I'VE HAD TO TAKE A WHITTLE TO MYSELF AND CARVE AWAY CHUNKS AND PARTS IN HOPES OF MAKING MYSELF MORE DIGESTIBLE. MANAGEABLE. EASIER TO HOLD. FOR SO LONG I HAVE FRAGMENTED MYSELF IN ORDER TO LET OTHERS FEEL POWERFUL,

ALL THE WHILE DIMINISHING THE POWER OF MY OWN WHOLENESS; THE RADIANCE THAT IS THE "AND-NESS" OF ME. LET ME BE THE INTERSECTION OF MY EXPERIENCES. LET ME BE LOUD AND LITTLE AND ALL THE REST.

I AM ALLOWED

I am allowed to rise to the sun's heat against my back
    Against my cheek
    The gentle caress of light and heat
    Reaching over and under and into me
    To sing and dance and collect the harvest
    Blooming endlessly around me
    Outfitting me in splendor and abundance
    I am allowed to rise to the sun's heat against my back
    Upon my womb
    The intense bursting of radiance
    Singing me into a new day
    A new season
    A singular moment in time yet in tandem with
    Something entirely more infinite
    In existence before time's first inhalation
    A melody of then, of now, of all that is
    yet to come

I am allowed—
    You are allowed, says the Sun
    To breathe and bathe and bask inside
    The light that is
    Yours
    Has always been
    Yours
    Rise and take your seat of play upon the earth
    Rise and take your seat of power upon the earth
    Rise and take your seat of rest upon the earth
    Rise and take your seat of smallness
    Of magnificence
    Of unnameable beauty
    Rise and let the hand of all that you have been -
    greet the hand of all that you are becoming

MARJIE MONRO

Emerge and meet the outstretched rays of your Destiny

——

I am allowed —
   I am allowed and I receive that —
   to rise with the sun's heat against my back
   To close my eyes and lose myself in its radiance
   With air filling my lungs and
   Tears leaking down my face
   Leap off the edge and into ecstasy
   With a laugh climbing up my throat and
   Bursting out to split the silence —
   Discover all that I already am
   And all that I am now becoming

ACKNOWLEDGMENTS

I would like to wholeheartedly thank LR, KB and JB, my dear friends and the very first readers of the words contained in these pages. Somehow the words *thank you* could never be enough. You have each been a friend to every iteration of me that has emerged on this journey of reclamation. You have been a safe place for me to grow into both my littleness and my power; soul mates to parts of me that at times felt entirely naked of companionship and naked of home. Thank you for seeing me clearly when my vision was hazy, for holding me up when my knees were wobbly and for believing in this book on those days I struggled to. Thank you, most of all, for allowing me to trust that no matter what happens next, I will always have a home with you.

ABOUT THE AUTHOR

Marjie Monro is a Nashville, TN based writer. In addition to writing, she is a Licensed Marriage and Family Therapist working primarily with clients with complex childhood trauma. Marjie is passionate about creating safe spaces for people to move out of stuck or aimless places toward new places of hope, healing, awareness, freedom and ultimately- connection.

Made in the USA
Middletown, DE
08 May 2023

30072338R00176